PRIVILEGED:

A Freshford Boyhood

Michael J. Lintern

EX LIBRIS PRESS

Published in 2015 by
Ex Libris Press
11 Regents Place
Bradford on Avon BA15 1ED

www.ex-librisbooks.co.uk

Printed by Print Essex, Colchester

ISBN 978-1-906641-87-0

© 2015 Michael J. Lintern

Contents

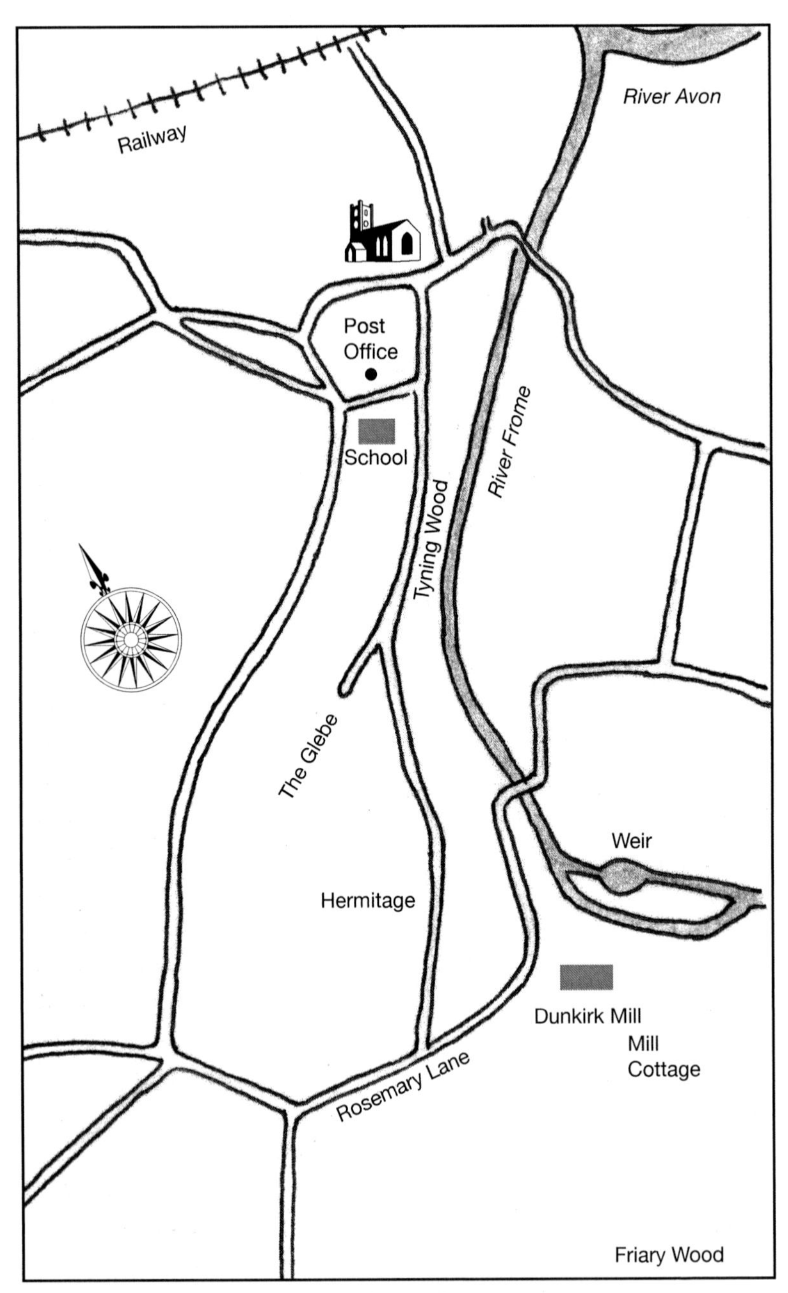

Freshford Village

Chapter 1

A Quiet Start

One's very early life is not easy to remember in detail but certain events, people and places will always be recalled by the impact they caused. I was, I believe, a very lucky young man. I always sensed a great deal of warmth and love surrounding me, not only from my Mum and Dad but also from their families, which remained constant for all of my young life and beyond.

I was born in Freshford cottage hospital a few miles from Westwood, the village where I spent the first eight years of my life. We were all working class but happy with it. In good families a child is usually protected, up to a point, from all the hardships of life and only comes to realise later the trials and tribulations that adults have to go through. I knew and accepted at first that Dad was absent for long periods of time. I just thought it was normal. What I didn't fully realise, but was probably told many times, was that he was in the army and away fighting for his country. I was born in 1941, the oldest of six. One thing that I can remember is being told with my younger brother Gerald, when we were old enough to walk, to go to the bottom end of Gran and Grandad's garden to wait for Dad. His joy at seeing us and hugging us was something that one could never forget. Coming from some foreign country and then travelling by train to Avoncliff Halt must have been a very happy journey for him, but to walk a mile or so across fields until he saw us two must have been so emotional for him. All the time he was away, along with letters for Mum, he would write small personal letters to me in coloured pencil and illustrated with drawings. In later years I was to see my efforts to him – they were not too impressive. I was privileged to have my father back safe and sound after the war.

Dad, Mum and me, November 1941

My Mum coped the best she could, the work and worry must have been horrendous for her at times. We stayed with her Mum and Dad for a few years until we moved into a house in the lower end of the village. Living with Gran and Grandad was no hardship, in fact it was a great deal of fun. Gran was great company and a good housewife and cook. All her water was carried to the house in buckets from a standpipe down the street and her cooking was done on a kitchen range fuelled by a coal fire in the living room. Watching her go about her business, even just watching and waiting for the kettle to boil or seeing how she did the cooking, proved a fascinating hobby for a young boy. Grandad was also a joy to be around, he never seemed to stop working. The garden was quite large and beautifully kept, it was a great playground. In the summer there were apples, plums, gooseberries and many other things to help ourselves to, within reason. One of the drawbacks was wasps; we soon learnt how angry they could get. Judy, the dog, also got our attention until she became bored and retreated to her favourite place to sleep. Grandad had built an air-raid shelter in the lawn by digging a large hole, constructing a room with old bedsteads and galvanised iron and then covering it with soil and turf. It made a great play area. Sometimes large bomber planes would pass over the house going from, and returning to, Colerne airfield which was some miles away, near Bath. I was warned to stay in the front porch but was allowed to look up to them as they passed overhead. The adults explained that it was in case something might drop off them and fall on me. It was pointed out to me that some of those returning planes had holes in them. As the flight path was over our house the sight and sounds became quite familiar and became a welcome diversion from the normal routine.

Grandad worked at the Royal Enfield engineering works at the stone quarry, at the far end of our road. In later years I was told that his only reply to family questions as to what he was working at was 'war work' and he would never say any more than that. In recent years it has been confirmed that the crown jewels and national works of art were stored in those caves. Grandad Taylor showed his skills at home by repairing bicycles, watches and clocks for members of the village community in his workshop attached to the house. The workshop also served as Judy's kennel and as garage for Grandad's vintage motorbike and sidecar. Now and again I had the great pleasure of going out for a trip with them, Gran in the sidecar and me riding pillion, grasping on tightly to Grandad. Motor cycle enthusiasts on spotting us would travel for miles not only watching us in action but also chatting to Grandad if we happened to stop. Gran showed a great deal of patience on these occasions.

One story that Mum told me in later years was that Queen Mary made a visit to the village during those war years. The population was informed that to see her they should congregate at the lower end of the village. On the day Mum, grandparents and neighbours set off. To Mum's consternation I chose that time to dirty my nappy, causing her to stay behind to change it. Mum's consolation was that as she passed the gates of the stone quarry, hurrying to get to the lower end of the village, a car drove out through the gates. To Mum's amazement and delight a window opened and Queen Mary gave the two of us a special royal wave and smile. Maybe she was visiting the crown jewels.

There was never a shortage of neighbours conversing with Gran and Grandad over the garden gate; maybe those hard times drew people together more. Certainly some households lost husbands and fathers. Mum's brother Alec was away fighting at the time, at least until he was made a prisoner of war. Her older sister Muriel had left to get married; she was my godmother and lived the other side of Bristol. My Uncle Alec could never bring himself to talk about his prison camp experience. I was lucky to be so young and innocent at that time but for my own good I was kept safe in the garden. I had to be content to watch the older children at play further down the street and was lucky enough to have the occasional chat with the odd one or two through the garden gate. One night a bat flew in through the open kitchen window while Gran was busy there. She immediately panicked. Grandad in his usual quiet manner said 'watch this' and turned the light off. The bat then got its bearings and flew out of the window. There was one great mystery about that place. Down in the garden was a hole in the ground, a tin bucket was sunk into the ground above it and all the household kitchen waste was poured into it. Mum said that all the years she had known it, it had never filled up. As there was the old stone quarry down the road maybe everything was finding its way into an abandoned part of the mine or perhaps into a fissure or cave.

Chapter 2

Making friends

Came the day of the move to Lower Westwood. I cannot remember who or how many took part, it just seemed a blur of activity as the horse and cart was loaded. There did seem to be a very full load and when all was finished I was placed on top of it. As the horse slowly set off with the neighbours waving us goodbye, my excitement gradually subsided as I began to wonder what was going to happen next. It helped that Mum and family were going with me. It was a bit strange at first but Mum's comforting hand soon worked its magic. The house I took in my stride but the big plus was a large garden at the back. My new playground had an apple tree, a small lawn and, best of all, a long path that took me up to the far end. It was there that I spent a large amount of time because I found the neighbour's chicken run next to the path. It was my first experience of chickens and I spent hours poking blades of grass through the wire but didn't find it easy avoiding their sharp beaks. It was wonderful to see the chickens running towards me as soon as I showed up. I never tired of feeding them their grass and they never tired of taking it. At least the lawn never needed cutting. In the spring I picked up apples off the lawn but the chickens never seemed interested in them so I floated them in next door's water butt.

On one of those days I was happily playing away when all of a sudden a creature came up from the depths and frightened the living daylights out of me. My first instinct was to run, which I did. The second one was to go back and touch it, which I did after summoning up a lot of courage. It didn't bite or savage me in any way, in fact I was disappointed when it went back down out of sight. I looked into the butt every day after that but rarely saw Mr Frog again. I did get an equally big surprise one day when Mr Cottle, the neighbour, suddenly appeared. He was an old man and looked a bit rough and tough but he soon put me at ease with his gentle manner. He asked me why I was looking into his tub, so I related my tale about the frog but expressed my puzzlement as to its non-appearance most of the time. Mr Cottle put his hand into the water and fished out the frog. To my utter astonishment it hopped out of his hand and off across the garden which gave us both quite a laugh. Mr Cottle was kind enough to chase and catch it and return it to the tub. He and I were then established good neighbours which gave me a feel-good factor.

Mum took my brother and me to visit Gran and Grandad regularly. It was a pleasant walk, they living at the top of the village and we at the bottom. One visit was unforgettable. Grandad had with all his skills built me a tricycle. It was a fantastic machine and I loved it to bits; it changed my life completely. I spent a lot of time haring up and down the garden path - the chickens were not amused. I did come to grief one day when the chain came off and I tried to put it back on myself. Unfortunately I managed to get my finger caught between the chain and the cog wheel. It was a very silly and extremely painful thing to do. Mum and a neighbour, after a great deal of patience and sweat, managed to save my finger. I never tried that again.

By this time another distraction had entered my life. We had a courtyard at the front of the house which gave me a new outlook on life. Through the wooden gate I was able some mornings to watch the young pupils go to school which was a little bit down the road on the other side. I loved to watch them all go in for the school assembly and loved to hear the hymns they sang. Two of those hymns have always been my favourites. They were a rowdy lot when they came out at the end of the day, so I kept well back from the gate. One of those lived at the Post Office a short way down the street but he went in by the back door so I was able to go along the back garden to wait for him. Although he was much older than me he was always approachable and he seemed a nice person. His name was Lawrence and Mum seemed to approve of him. However, all good things come to an end and one day he told me he was leaving. What I didn't know was that Lawrence was a wartime evacuee and was now going back to London to his Mum and Dad. I didn't understand at first and quite missed him for a while. Although it was him that caused the chain to come off the trike, I felt it was just an accident.

Now and then, when their busy lives allowed, members of both of my parents' families paid us visits. One of those was Aunt Beat, short for Beatrice, who was actually Mum's aunt, being her mother's sister. She always arrived on her bicycle which had a basket on the front which usually contained a useful household present for us. She had cycled about three miles to get to us and one of the good things we liked about her visit was the treats we sometimes found in her basket. During the exceptionally hard winter of 1947 Auntie rode her bicycle to us through all the heavy ice and snow. It left me with a feeling that I must try that one day. Another regular visitor was Dad's sister Aunt May. Although I didn't realise at the time Mum was suffering from war depression. I am not surprised, she must have suffered agonies not knowing if the man she loved would survive the dangers of war and return safely to us. It could explain why Mum and I would just sit quietly for long periods in front of the fire in silence. Even then all was not entirely still. A regular visitor would be a mouse that would come under the coal store cupboard door which was right next to the fire grate. We watched fascinated as the mouse slowly came along until it was between us and the fire, looking for crumbs dropped from any food we may have been eating. Our imitation of statues either fooled him or he realised that we meant him no harm. Aunt May stayed weekends in support of Mum and I remember how well they got on. The world would be a better place if we all helped each other so well.

I think my love of nature and the creatures that lived in

the wild grew from that time. The day arrived when I became old enough to go to school, whether I liked it or not. After watching those rumbustious children entering and spilling out of the place, I was more than a bit nervous at the prospect. The fact that I was a bit shy coupled with the fact that, except for my classmates, all the other boys and girls were bigger than me must have put me on my guard. Not being able to cope with lessons too well, I must have in my mind decided enough is enough. Every day I went home Mum asked me what I had done that day. My reply was always 'Nothing'. After a while she became curious and a bit worried so she went across to the school at classtime. Sure enough, there I sat at my desk with my arms folded and my mouth firmly shut in a determined fashion. Teacher told her that was how I spent most of the day and no end of encouragement seemed to make any difference. Mum told her, 'leave it to me'. On arriving home she gave me a good talking to which took the brakes off and gave me a new outlook on life. I found joining was quite good fun and lessons became easier. I also made good friends with my classmates which I had been worried about.

Westwood School

Life has a nasty way of hurting; I found that out quite early. One day one of our classmates did not turn up. We were told later in the day that she would not be coming back as she had been killed in an accident. She was blond with a bubbly personality and I had got on particularly well with her. Although we were all very young and didn't fully understand the situation, it had a lot of us in tears. The lane to the cemetery passed the back end of the school and on the day of the funeral the school went quiet. I don't know what the seniors did in their half of the school but we juniors stood on chairs and watched in silence as the coffin went slowly by. It's something one never forgets. I found out later from Mum that she had been kicked in the head by a horse when she got too close to it. Her parents were family friends. In later years another classmate, a boy, was killed when a horse chestnut tree was struck by lightning whilst he was sheltering underneath it during a storm. My parents drummed into me how dangerous lightning could be.

With the arrival of my sister Jean came the added pleasure of playing in the baby's bath water in the tin bath on the kitchen table. Times were changing all around for me: I was having to learn to share with brother Gerald, new baby Jean took centre stage, school was my new experience and then, joy of joys, Dad returned home safely from the war. Space was becoming limited in that small house. My brother and I slept in the top bedroom and baby Jean slept in the lower one with Mum and Dad. I didn't really appreciate how primitive it all was until we moved to a council house in later years. I know there was no electricity in the house and I can't remember if we had gaslight. There was a gas stove but no running water, every drop had to be carried from a standpipe down the street. It worked well enough in normal times but, in the winter's most

March 1945, myself, Jean and Dad

freezing cold weather when the standpipe froze, a container with boiling hot water had to be used by the first person to go there in the morning to thaw it out. It meant that a certain amount of water had to be kept by for this purpose. I used to watch Mum fill the brick-built boiler up in the kitchen, light a wood fire underneath and take the clothes out of the boiling hot washing water with a large 'copper stick' when it was finished. After rinsing in the sink and running it through the mangle, she hung the washing out to dry in the garden. It makes me feel quite guilty nowadays when I push the button on the washing machine.

VE-Day at Lower Westwood, Michael, Jean and Mum

When Dad arrived home it was a bit strange at first but gradually we all felt at ease with each other. Dad worked so hard to improve our lot, in the house and garden but he did make one mistake as far as I was concerned. By this time our mouse had a wife and family (or husband and family) and Dad was not happy with that. He put down traps for the vermin who were by now raiding the larder. I came in from the garden and spotted my mouse friends dead in the traps. Poor Dad was now in a no-win situation. Despite his best efforts, I wouldn't stop crying so, in desperation, he locked me out in the garden until I shut up. A few days later I thought I had the chance to get my own back. Dad had gone to the outside toilet while I was playing outside. Seizing the chance with both hands, I dropped the latch on the door. When Dad had finished, he tried to come out but, try as he might, he couldn't open the door. As he had started to shout a bit, I nipped off quick into the house. It was quite a while before he was heard and let out and by then his kettle was well and truly boiling. I was very wrong to think that revenge was sweet. After admitting I was the culprit, I found myself locked in the garden shed for a while as punishment. It happened to me a few times after that until I realised who really was in charge.

When not at school I still enjoyed feeding and talking to the neighbour's chickens, trying not to frighten them on my trike. The frog seemed to have disappeared. My new adventure was freedom outside the front of the house. As I had started school and knew that discipline was important, I was allowed to play with the other children in the street. It was impressed on me that I was not to go beyond the pavement at each end of the street. The other children also bided by that rule but we all enjoyed our situation. It was amazing how many things took our interest, not least the farm at the top end of the street. Unfortunately it was on the other side of the road so we had to watch from afar. A herd of cows passing us on their way for milking was an interesting but sometimes smelly happening. Tractors came and went but the thing that kept us interested was the brightly coloured bantams that tended to wander out of the gate. They would wander up and down the grass kerbside pecking away but, no matter how hard we tried, we could never encourage them to come down nearer to us.

There was a patch of waste ground between the houses halfway down the street, it must have been someone's garden a long time ago as flowers still grew wild amongst the grass. There was a lilac tree and blue periwinkle had spread everywhere which my friend David Farley and I picked and took home. We also made good use of the standpipe in the hot weather as well as the phone box, though we were warned off by concerned adults. There were about eight of us but Kenneth, Margaret, David and I were all about the same age. One of them brought out some marbles one day. It really took off and we would spend hours honing our skills up and down the street. Even though I had none, the others were quite happy to let me use theirs. We were a happy bunch. We were quite safe playing all over the road as not much traffic seemed to go through the village.

At haymaking time the farmer's horse and cart would go up the street with the hay piled very high. We were glued to its progress because as it passed the farm entrance on its way to the back gate, we all held our breath. The road entrance was dipped and the pile of hay would lean at an alarming angle. It always seemed a bit of a miracle that everything stayed upright. Another horse and cart, an everyday one, was driven by Tom Walsh the milkman. He owned a farm at the bottom end of the village and took his milk all round the village in milk churns. I would watch as he measured out the milk from his long handled scoop, which hooked onto the inside of his churn, into Mum's jug. He must have worked a very long day.

I bonded best with David who lived at the top end house. I only had to ask 'could I go out to play with David' and the gate was opened and I was scampering up the street like a rabbit. Children will fall out and sometimes fight, so inevitably did David and I, but not very often. One incident stood out for its humour. We had a difference of opinion which escalated into us trying to knock six bells out of one another. Outside David's house was a tin bath, kept at the bottom of the rainwater downpipe. Its water was used in the house and garden to save a tiresome walk to the standpipe. On this occasion the bath was full but David and I never noticed until we fell into it. The shock stopped all conflict and fear took over. Some of David's family heard the crash of the empty bath and came rushing out. 'Now I'm in trouble' I thought. To the relief of us both, David's family went from being a bit annoyed about the loss of their water to bursting into laughter, as we stood there like drowned rats.. On hearing the noise some of the neighbours came out. Their reaction was the same. I couldn't get home fast enough.

David also had a wicked sense of humour as I found out on a certain Sunday afternoon. Dad had very kindly brought home two pet rabbits, black in colour. Their hutch was put at the end of the garden next to the chicken run so I spent a lot of time there. I wasn't content to just look at them or feed them grass through the wire mesh so I would open the door, take them out and give them a cuddle. Unfortunately I forgot to close the door afterwards on one occasion and they went missing. On the following Sunday afternoon David was out in his back garden a few doors away and, on seeing me, shouted out that they had just eaten a good Sunday dinner, adding it was the rabbits they had found wandering in their back garden. Mum and Dad said 'don't believe him, it's not true'. It was only many years later that I found out Dad had found my pets eating a neighbour's lettuces and took them back to where he bought them as a precaution from future escapes.

The spirit of adventure became too much for us one day when we were told by other children that they knew of a pond in a field. Fired up with curiosity off we all trooped. First we looked and then we paddled a bit and by the time we got home we were covered in mud. Needless to say, our parents were a bit upset and we were all kept indoors for a while. On one momentous day my brother Gerald became upset and angry about something that had happened in our house and stormed out declaring to us that he was going to leave home. We watched as he marched up to the end of the street and disappeared around the bend. After a while, when he didn't reappear, I went and passed on the news to Mum. 'He's leaving home is he', she said, 'I will see about that' and she also disappeared at the end of the street. After a while waiting they both came into sight at as good a pace, poor Gerald in front crying and Mum behind stinging his legs with a stick. He never did that again.

Michael and Gerald, Upper Westwood, June 1945

Now Dad was back he would walk my brother and I up to my Gran and Grandad's house at the top of the village on a Sunday morning. As soon as we got there Grandad would take me for a walk up the lane just as he had when we lived there. He had been my stand-in father whilst Dad was away. It felt just like going home and I loved those two so much. On our walk we would, depending on the time of year, sometimes pick flowers, eat nuts and blackberries or just watch birds. If we found a bird's nest it would be fun to watch the progress involved. It was a routine that I looked forward to and loved. Another part of the routine was to get a sweet or two from a wooden hinged box that Gran kept on a shelf halfway up the stairs. Another treat was to stand in front of their radio and listen in wonder; it was the first one I had ever seen. Grandad tried to explain how it worked but the science of the accumulator and very large battery was like water off a duck's back. Grandad also played the upright piano. He was self-taught, never having had a day's lesson in his life. Mum told me that he had entertained her, her brother, sister and Gran with his singing and playing. Their favourite was 'Gee up horsey, don't you stop, just let your feet go clippety clop'. There were still trips on the motor bike and sidecar to enjoy. One was to Farleigh Hungerford motor cycle grass track. It involved a lot of noise, thrill and spills and a picnic as well. We enjoyed going to watch Trowbridge Carnival procession every year. To me those early years with Gran and Grandad were golden.

My second sister Carolyn arrived and Dad, as usual, was doing his best. He had found a job in the village as a gardener for Mr Thurston. My brother and I would meet him outside the grounds and walk home with him. On the first Guy Fawkes night that I can remember Dad's sense of humour went overboard. He made a guy as big as himself, stuffing his old clothes with rolled up newspapers. He even had gloves, a hat and a lifelike face drawn on the white paper bag that was his head. The first we knew about it was when we three children were lined up in the kitchen facing the outside door. Dad then left us, went out of the front door and around the back. After a short wait there was a knock on the scullery door. I undid the latch, being the only one that could reach it, and then stepped back. To our horror, a huge lifelike figure filled the doorway; in fact it seemed to tower over us. A voice seemed to come from this huge apparition, of course it was Dad's. My brother and I were petrified and rooted to the floor; we couldn't have moved, I don't think, even if we had wanted to. Poor little toddler Jean ran screaming into the front room to Mum. It took a long time to calm her down. Peace was restored after a while but it did not help our sister to see Guy Fawkes in the bonfire on bonfire night. Gerald and I soon got over our fears. We saw the joke as it was intended and for years after always tried to make a Guy as Dad had done, for his part Dad always helped to make bonfire night a success.

School in the meantime was going well. A school band had been started up and my class were encouraged to take part. I don't remember how we sounded, there must have been some pupils who were coping. All I can remember was a lot of jumbled sound and a lot of enthusiasm. My instrument was the triangle, a lot of talent there! On one memorable occasion a marching band came down our street. We heard it coming and I and other children followed it down to the end of the road. There I stopped but to my surprise some of the others did not. They followed those bandsmen in their brightly coloured uniforms and were soon out of sight. Later on, the parents of those children enquired of us where they were. The next thing we knew was those parents following suit. The rumour was that the band was going to Trowbridge. I was glad I was not in those children's shoes for Trowbridge was about three miles away and the distance was not going to be their only problem that day.

Coach trips were organised in the village and one of those I have never forgotten. We were bowling along, I was in the second coach, when we came to some other coaches parked by the side of the road so that their passengers could take a toilet break in the nearby wooded area. Our coach had just gone around one of those parked vehicles when it suddenly happened. A young girl ran down the bank on the left hand side of the road, directly into the path of the coach in front of ours. It happened so quickly, she was going so fast, the driver did not stand a chance of stopping. My vision of it to this day is just so clear as if it only happened yesterday. She was a beautiful blond girl of about eight, nine or ten, it was difficult to tell. As she ran down the bank with long blond hair and long pure white dress following behind her all those who saw it knew what was about to happen. As she disappeared behind the front of the coach I could see her feet going along underneath and then she was hit on the driver's side. Nothing was spared our gaze as first the front wheel went over her and then the back. The coach stopped and then carried on up the road for a short way and then parked, ours followed. As we passed the stricken girl, I looked down at her as I was sat next to the window on her side. She lay there on her back with her eyes shut and blood was just starting to come from her mouth. After a long wait in which nobody was allowed to leave the coach, we children were made to sit down and not look back and our coach was allowed on its way. We actually went on to the seaside but I don't think anybody enjoyed themselves. On the way home our coach stopped at the hospital where she had been taken and someone went in. When they came back, their faces were very grim and I overheard the words, 'every bone in her body'. I have tried in recent years to find somebody who could perhaps tell me if she had lived or died, without success. I can forget about it for a while, sometimes years, then something will happen and my mind will receive a flashback.

The winter of 1947, when I was six years old, was a notoriously bad one. My childish impression of it was first of all amazement at the height of the snow and snowdrifts, and then the sheer constant coldness of it. Icicles hung from everything, big long ones. School was not cancelled; it was probably warmer there than inside some of the homes. To get to the outside toilets, trenches were dug in the snow. As we young ones walked through them, the snow towered above us. Were we worried? Of course not, it was fun. For the adults it must have been so hard. Without the modern conveniences of our day, such as central heating, hot and cold running water, snowploughs, salted road grit, etc., it must have been a very tiring and uphill battle.

At Freshford, the village a few miles away where I was born, every road in and out was a steep hill. Mill Cottage, Dad's family home there, was still occupied by his five brothers, one sister who was younger than him, and Gran and Grandad Lintern. Like Dad, who had been called up to fight soon after his marriage, my uncles Bob, Harold and Fred also returned safely from the war. Uncle Harold had re-started his smallholding farm which was near enough to Mill Cottage that the family could easily help Uncle out with small jobs when he became hard pressed. Dad used to take Gerald and me to visit his family on a Saturday so Mum could have some time off from the strain of four youngsters. The whole place was a bit like heaven to me but the journey could be a bit tiring at times. To get us to Mill Cottage with just his bicycle Dad certainly had to use his ingenuity. For my younger brother he fixed a saddle onto the crossbar and a wooden spar across the lower bar for Gerald to rest his feet. For me he had a long rope that stretched from his saddle to the front of my tricycle. I had always thought that I was very speedy on my machine until those rides to Freshford and back. Dad later said that my little legs went round like pistons but I never complained. Little did he know that I would lift my legs up from the pedals and let them spin round, only putting them back on when Dad looked round to check I was alright.

It was about this time Dad's sister Aunt May was struck down by polio. After all her kindnesses to Mum, who had been unwell with depression while Dad was away, it seemed so unfair and cruel. She was in hospital for seven months and came out with her right leg paralysed. Despite physiotherapy and all the attempts to help by Gran and her sister, Aunt Annie, , she never got the feeling back. Aunt May's cheerful and upbeat nature probably got her through those dark days.

Chapter 3

Off Elsewhere

In 1949 Mum was expecting another baby so to help out, me and Gerald were sent to stay with Auntie Muriel and Uncle Fred who lived at Backwell Farleigh on the other side of Bristol. Auntie Muriel was my godmother as well as Mum's sister and I remember visiting her house when I was younger. Since that visit with Mum though, Auntie Muriel and Uncle Frank had moved and they now had a son, Marcus. The new house was a tied cottage in the grounds of a large house where Uncle was the gardener.

When we arrived there we realised we were somewhere special. Auntie Muriel and Uncle Fred were kindness itself and we discovered that Marcus, although he was much younger than us, was more than pleased to have two new playmates. As long as we didn't trespass into the immediate area around the big house we had the freedom of the estate. There was an invisible line that we were warned not to cross and we didn't. Our area was a young boy's paradise. There was a swing hanging from the trees halfway down the main drive that we could use if we wanted to. We took full advantage of that. There were apple, plum, medlar and nut trees and we had arrived at just the right time for those fruits and nuts. The only problem was the wasps; there was an awful lot of them. Medlars were a favourite of mine and still are. There was an abundance of birds, amongst them the woodpeckers who were in trees up by the big house. We could see and hear them; their loud drilling seemed to fill the air at times.

What we didn't realise was that when the summer school holidays came to an end we were expected to go to school. What an emotional shock that was. Once again we were some of the smallest and youngest in the school, which was also a senior school, and the boys were much more active and aggressive than at Westwood Junior and Infants. The school was at Nailsea so to get there Auntie Muriel took us to a waiting area in the village; later we made our own way there to catch the school bus. The other half dozen waiting boys were much older than us and had the devil in them. They were mischievous pranksters but not vicious. We were permanently on our guard but never came to any harm. It made for a lively trip there and back. The cheekiest of the bunch was a boy with the surname of Cutler whose family owned the garage in the village. Much later when he left the school he formed a Country and Western group that became quite famous, making hit records. They were called Adge Cutler and the Wurzels and Adge's fun loving style shone through, reminding me of those days. When it was clear we were going back home he got very friendly and asked a lot of questions as to what our area was like.

Once we arrived at school the real stress started. It was a different world. There always seemed to be a fight going on in the playground and if somebody said 'boo' to me I would jump a mile. Auntie had bought me a cap which resembled a deerstalker. Some of the other boys thought it would be funny to use it first as a football, then a rugby ball, laughing at my efforts to get it back. It was quite a job to get it back into shape before I got home. My moment of glory came unexpectedly in the school assembly one morning. Somebody was misbehaving at the back of the room where the bigger boys sat. The headmaster's response was to pick up a wicker wastepaper basket at the front of the hall and vigorously throw it at the trouble area. Before it got there, it bounced off my head and dropped just behind me. We had been singing a hymn and all of use, including me, carried on to the end. I do remember the silence afterwards when a very concerned and apologetic headmaster asked me, more than once, if I was okay. The incident got me excused from morning lessons and by the time I went back in the afternoon I had suddenly become popular. It turned out to be my moment of salvation. I was a bit surprised at the number of pupils who went out of their way to be friendly to me and kept me away from trouble when fights broke out but my hat now stayed on my head. Gerald and I found the larking about was toned down on our travels to and from school too. We were quite loathe to leave when the time came.

Cousin Marcus was too young to have started school but was always glad when we came home and spent some playtime with him. One of our favourite games was to race round an apple tree in the orchard next to the house, pretending to be racing car drivers. I often wondered afterwards if the grass grew again because when we left it had turned into a dirt track. I think Aunt and Uncle turned a blind eye because we never had any trouble going to sleep at night. One thing that I did miss was my walk with Uncle Fred. On previous visits before I was of school age, they lived in another house down in the village. Uncle and I would wander down the lane where the great attraction was a brook running beside the road. It held an endless fascination for me. We watched small fish, ducks, rabbits in the field and ate blackberries. Unfortunately lack of time and circumstance made it one pleasure that I had to forego. Aunt Muriel was my godmother and on my third birthday gave me a magnificent bible which I still read occasionally.

All good things must come to an end so home we had to go. I said goodbye to young Mr Cutler on a Sunday morning at the entrance to the estate's driveway. He seemed genuinely sorry to see me go. It gave me a feel-good factor and made me also feel that our time there was not wasted. I am not surprised that Adge went on to make such a success of his life, especially if he showed such a keen interest in other people and places. He used his God-given talent in the right way and country music was the benefactor. I was obviously told beforehand what to expect going home but it still came as a bit of a blow to find that home was new. Not only a new house on a small estate, the Glebe where some of the houses had not even been finished, but also in a new village. On top of that I now had a new sister, Julia.

Chapter 4

A New Home

No matter how well I may have been warned about the coming changes, my reaction was to be worried and go quiet for a while. Freshford village was where I had now landed, just a few miles from Westwood where I had spent my early years. Freshford was the village of my birth. Westwood seemed light years away and I wasn't sure about the change. I couldn't remember saying goodbye to all my friends, maybe didn't really believe it was all going to happen. My brother and three sisters helped to soften the blow and Mum and Dad's happiness with the house made for a happy family feeling. I wasn't fully aware of the huge benefits that Mum and Dad were experiencing at the time but later in life I became aware when I was told. Pressing a switch and getting electric light was sheer pleasure. There was now hot water from the immersion heater too but the jewel in the crown was the water taps. Mum couldn't get over the fact that all she had to do was turn the tap and there it was. At first she said it was like Christmas three times over. On top of these luxuries there were two toilets inside the house and a proper bath. After all the years of hardship Mum openly enjoyed it, full stop. Things had worked out well, thank goodness, and life had a lot in store for me.

We had lots of visits from relatives to view our new palace and the new baby who was great until she cried. One of those was Dad's brother Uncle Fred who had brought me a wind-up gramophone to our old home, a wonderful gesture as it introduced me to music for the first time and I loved it. I had spent hours listening to George Formby records amongst others. Unfortunately the gramophone's spring had broken and, try as he might, Grandad Taylor could not repair it.

We never went out of the house much, just played together as a family and sometimes watched the builders working on the other unfinished houses. One day, when my brother and I were having a punch-up over some disagreement, we were startled by a couple of noisy youngsters going down the path outside. They were the first young children our age we had seen on the estate. Our first reaction was to duck down below the level of the window; our second was, what are we were afraid of? Over the next few days we watched from a distance in the house until we were sure they were okay. We were then asked to be let out. Our parents guessed why and away we went. We were lucky to have Robert and Eileen Kay as next door neighbours. They were two of the nicest people one could wish to meet and they made the place buzz. My friendship with Robert has lasted all our lives.

As the rest of the sixteen houses gradually filled up, more youngsters moved in. For me it was Westwood all over again. We were all ages, shapes and sizes but a really good band was formed. My tricycle was very popular but there were only two bicycles to be had. Bobbie Rose owned the other one but it was a two wheeler and at first nobody could ride it, so we did the best we could with it. Mobility became the burning passion as one by one we made trolleys. We scrounged flat pieces of wood for the body and then old pram wheels. The front axle had a length of wood nailed to it and a single bolt in the middle joined it to the main body. Add a length of rope or thick string tied to each side of the front axle, steer with your feet and you were away. The only snag was it only ran downhill. As we were all good friends we took turns in pushing each other. It could be a very tiring game. Our way around the hard labour was to race them down hill. The best hill was the short but quite steep one leading out of the estate. The problem with this plan was the Tyning road going along the bottom which our hill fed into. Someone had to be down there to check if the road was clear. When the right signal was given, off we would go. That was one exciting ride not only for the speed but two or three going together made it quite hairy. Collisions were commonplace resulting in many scrapes but no broken bones ever happened. As we got more proficient a certain manoeuvre was tried. On getting to the bottom of the hill at full speed a sharp turn to the left was tried taking us round the war memorial on grass. My worst and last try at that dopey manoeuvre was one where I lost control and rubbed along the barbed wire fence that bordered the next door field. My shirt and vest were ripped off my chest and I was damaged by the barbed wire. Being told how stupid I had been was nearly as bad as my injuries. I played safe after that.

At the bottom of the hill on the other side of the road was a huge conker tree which, when the tree was full in the autumn, was attacked by every small boy in the area. It was so tall nobody could throw a stick or stone anywhere near the top. We enjoyed trying to knock the conkers down as much as we did using them. One day we discovered some large stones that were once part of a fallen wall near the tree. The wood stretched from the conker tree at the top right down to the River Frome at the bottom. It was a very steep drop. The temptation was too much for a gang of small boys. We sent those stones off down that hill hoping to hear them splash into the river below. Some of them hit trees on the way down but some reached their destination. What we had forgotten was the public footpath alongside the river. My Gran Lintern was making her way to the shops up that path when those huge stones came whistling down through the trees. She went back and then straight up to the police station. We had almost run out of ammunition and were thinking of going home when a voice hailed us and a policeman came out of the wood a short distance away. It was one almighty shock, we knew we were in deep trouble when he explained to us how dangerous our actions were and a woman on the path was lucky to get away unhurt. He didn't tell us it was my Gran; Mum and Dad told me later after the policeman had paid a visit. My personal punishment was to go and apologise to Gran but our joint punishment was worse, much worse.

Mr Rossiter was an extremely shrewd, wise man and probably understood us very well as he had two sons of his own, Peter and Tony. Instead of threatening us with lawful proceedings or taking action in that respect, he took us down to the river at the bottom of the wood. In a very stern manner he told us that every one of those stones was to be taken back up to the top, even those in the river, and we weren't going until we had finished. There was no choice, we were guilty and so the struggle began. Those stones were big and we were relatively small but that wood was so steep it looked like mission impossible. I am not sure how many, if any, of those stones actually reached the top. After a long while we got to the point of desperation, not only were we very tired but our best efforts were getting us nowhere. We were not up to the job and one or two of us started to cry, me included. Mr Rossiter did have a heart and on seeing us at the end of our tether, let us off with a warning as to our future behaviour. We never stepped outside the law again; Mr Rossiter was always at the back of our minds. Mr and Mrs Rossiter ran a fish and chip shop in the village and in future years I was able to see our village constable in a much happier light.

From the very start, when we had all moved in, the elder boys took us under their wings. They were local boys and knew the village well, we learnt a lot from them. One game they played and let us join in was called tracking. It involved two teams and Tyning Wood and for safety's sake we did it in pairs. One team would leave the large conker tree and arrows were made of twigs for the tracking team to follow. At a suitable distance away the letter 'H' for home would be formed and the first team would have to try and get back to the conker tree without the following team catching them. They would have to touch the tree before the person left guarding the tree touched them. It was a great game we all enjoyed and could take a long time from beginning to end. In the estate, Philip who lived next door to us was successful in organising races around the paths. He did it as a handicap race by giving the youngest the shortest distance to run and staggered the starting distances according to age. Philip and his older friends along with some from the village started up cycle racing at the lower end of Tyning field which was near to the estate. We enjoyed watching them, they were very competitive and stirred something inside us. The trouble was none of us could ride a two-wheeler but necessity is the mother of invention. We came up with the bright idea that our race track at the top of Tyning field would involve bowling bicycle tyres or wheels, anything we could find, just to satisfy our competitive natures. Philip, David, Mick and others from the village probably never realised how much we appreciated the time they spent on us younger generation and how it helped our initial bonding.

On one occasion I was walking up the footpath in Tyning Wood when a voice spoke to me. Turning round I couldn't see a soul. It spoke to me several times again. I was absolutely perplexed and probably looked it. After having his bit of fun, Mick stepped out from behind a large tree, a short distance away with a big grin on his face. I relaxed, told him he had me completely fooled and joined in the laughter. As I tried to climb up the steep bank towards him, I found I was slipping and sliding all over the place. On seeing this, he showed me that by digging my feet sideways into the bank and putting my full weight on them I was in complete control of the situation. I was able to pass it on to my friends.

I was happy to divide my time between Dad's family home, Mill Cottage and my estate friends. The majority of the week was taken up with my education at the village school. I was no longer an infant but was now a junior. This meant that I was in the top class that Mrs Dicks taught. She was an unforgettable character, never short of praise and encouragement, very observant but quick to clamp down on any bad behaviour. She was a big-built woman but very quiet on her feet in class; one never knew where she was. If she noticed somebody messing about instead of working, she sometimes would hit the culprit on the knuckles with a metal ruler that she picked up from another desk. The sudden shock was as bad as the pain, it paid to behave oneself. She was very keen on physical education and we welcomed the challenges she gave us. We became so good that after a school inspector visited us, he not only gave us top marks but we got new daps to wear as a reward. Mrs Dicks' praise made us all feel good and she made a point of encouraging our bookwork, spending individual time with us all. She told me she had taught my father. He had a love of nature and she had noticed that I had too. I realised how true it was and, from that moment on, a part of my life has been spent in appreciating the birds, animals, trees and fields. Just being on my own in a quiet part of the countryside has given me enormous pleasure and peace of mind. I take that experience when the opportunity arises with both hands and pine if it doesn't happen often enough.

Somerset Education Committee.

Freshford V.C. Junior School.

Report for Half Year ending July 27th 1951.

MICHAEL LINTERN.

SCRIPTURE	Good.
ARITHMETIC	Fairly Good.
ENGLISH	Very Good.
PHYSICAL EDUCATION	Very Good.
NATURE STUDY	Excellent.
GEOGRAPHY	Very Good
HISTORY.	Very Good.

Michael is a studious child, who is very interested in his work.

D. E. Dicks.

The other boys and girls at that school were great. Our community was so strong we sometimes played our games in the playground as a whole. The icing on my cake was visiting Mill Cottage and Uncle's farm. We couldn't go there during our school week but Saturdays came round just like a weekly holiday. Gran and Dad's siblings had always showed our family a great deal of loving kindness and we were made to feel welcome when we visited Mill Cottage; nothing had changed. Because Grandad had died of flu at the relatively early age of 55 leaving Gran with six children to bring up, they had become a very hard working, resourceful and united family. Gran herself set the example for her children. One of her enterprises was to serve tea and refreshments in the front garden in the summer to visitors to the nearby river and weir. The area around the Mill Cottage was, and still is, a real beauty spot and no doubt Gran's refreshments were a welcome to the many summer trippers. The children, when they were old enough, found casual part-time employment in the village.

Mill Cottage was actually Dunkirk Mill Cottage as it was attached to a large derelict mill, Dunkirk Mill, which had been built for the woollen industry. It became quite dangerous because slates were coming off the abandoned mill's roof letting the water in and the roof was collapsing because of the timbers deteriorating. The family story goes that one night there was such a huge collapse it shook the cottage next door and woke everybody up. They thought for a moment that the Germans had dropped a bomb and then realised that the war had ended some years ago. Some of those fallen timbers were in danger of rotting away, causing damage to Mill Cottage or damage to anybody who entered the place, so the Uncles made good use of them. They were taken out, cut into chumps, split into kindling fire wood and then sold in bags. Anybody who had time to spare would sit on a large log of wood and chop those chumps up. I took my turn and quite enjoyed it, except when I hit a finger. Luckily the chopper was never razor sharp but one became very skilful very quickly.

My brother and I were warned to take great care around the

Mill Cottage, June 1940, from above

Mill Cottage (now Mill House), Dunkirk Mill, Freshford c. 1960

old derelict mill and never to go up the flight of stairs that led to the upper floors. We did our share of wandering around in there but after a while it became a bit boring. That flight of stairs was so tantalising. Boys will be boys and eventually our curiosity go the better of us and up we went. The stair timber was quite old and not only looked but felt unsafe. Nevertheless we made it up to the first floor and looked through the doorway. The room was very large; the floorboards looked unsafe with holes in them caused by the ravages of time and woodworm. Some debris from the fallen roof was poking through from the floor above and some had come to rest on the floor. It looked a very dangerous place to go but it was a challenge to two small boys. We soon found out what all the fuss was about as we stupidly crept across those boards. The inevitable happened. Those rotten boards would not take even our weight; they started breaking up and then one of my legs went through and downwards. Fortunately I pulled my leg out of that hole, we both scampered back to the stairs and went slowly down. We never went up there again.

Dunkirk Mill was built by Thomas Joyce as a woollen mill in 1795 and ceased trading in 1912 when it was abandoned; its long hard life was now showing. It was covered in ivy and in certain parts by a creeper commonly known as Old Man's Beard because of the flower it produced. One of the uncles showed us that if we could find a dead, dried piece of creeper and snapped off a short length, we could set light to one end and smoke it like a cigar. The sheer novelty of it amused my brother and me but we were warned not to overdo it. Not sure what that meant, we decided to find a private place. There was a gap between the old mill and a footpath that went around the back and in those days there were no council refuse collections so the gap was used as the family's rubbish dump. My brother and I found that it was suspended on creeper and ivy branches and we found plenty of room underneath, the perfect place for a smoke. When my brother and I went down to Mill Cottage on a Saturday morning we detoured a bit and went down the steep Rosemary lane that led there. Growing wild on the bank at the side of the road was a plant called lemon balm which, when rubbed between one's hands, gave off a lovely lemon aroma. We would pick some and present it to Aunt May who had arrived home from her long, difficult and worrying stay in hospital. She had survived her illness, polio, but was left with a paralysed leg and was bed bound to start with. Auntie's cheerful upbeat nature had got her through it but the uncertainty of her future must have got her down at times. We hoped our small present and visits helped a little and we certainly enjoyed her company.

Dunkirk Mill, Freshford, c. 1960

The whole experience of going down there was amazing. Dad's family were a constant source of interest to me sometimes amusement and definitely an education. Mill Cottage with Gran in charge was the centre of all that took place. Gran was a very strong character, having to care and try to help her six children when Grandad died much too early must have been so hard for her. Maybe all pulling together helped to ease her burden somewhat. Her experience with her own brood must have made it easy to keep us two small boys on the straight and narrow. Amongst her many capabilities she had one talent that impressed us all. Uncle's farm being next to the house and the large back gardens all within calling distance, Gran had everybody who was around the area in her front room when the time came for a mid-day break. Gran never wasted her breath and time shouting to all four corners. No, Gran had a bugle. She blew it loud and clear and nobody could fail to hear it. I tried for many years to make a good call on that bugle but could never equal Gran's. Those mid-day breaks were memorable, everything that concerned the family was discussed, no problem was left if not solved, well chewed through. Any rebukes for stepping out of line were given to us as well but never in a heavy handed manner. The thing I liked best was the stories from the past that were either unusual or amusing. They were obviously related for my benefit. It cemented my relationship with my family and I have always been proud of being a Lintern.

Gran had a beautiful cat called Fluffy. You only had to look at her to know how she had got her name. The only other cats around were Uncle's farm cats and nature being what it is, she came home pregnant now and then. She always had her litter where she slept in a small cupboard next to the fireplace. Her trust in me was so good that she would let me take them out for a short time after they were born. They would still be blind and could only crawl. We would play with them for a short while and then hand them back to their anxious mum. Gran would always help Uncle whenever she could with farm matters, especially at Christmas time when there were a lot of chickens to pluck. On arriving there one day there was a box in front of the fire. It held a huge surprise for, on looking inside, there lay a baby pig. The explanation was that its mother had accidentally rolled on it and they didn't know if it would recover. I can't remember the outcome but I was never surprised at what I might find in Mill Cottage again.

Just like our old home at Westwood there was no running water at Mill Cottage. The source for that valuable commodity was about a hundred yards or more down the lane. The pathway from the lane went down the river bank on an angle until it reached a well, built horizontally under the river bank. The water was pure and clear as it came from the back of the bank and ran out into the river. Mum has told me that my baby bottles were made up with it so it must have been hygienic. The hard part was carrying it up to the cottage in buckets. There was a table with four buckets on, always kept full. I was allowed to help when they found a half-size bucket. It must have been difficult when the weather was bad and I often wonder how they coped when the river was flooded.

To start with I was taken round the farm just for viewing purposes but, as I got older and stronger, Uncle found me small jobs to do which I enjoyed tremendously. My inquisitive mind and adventurous spirit were inspiring me to wander off exploring at times. The family knew how dangerous that could be for a small boy like me and it was difficult to keep an eye on me all the time, nevertheless I did manage to get away at times. When they found I had been down to the river or up into Friary Wood Gran or one of the others would take me there, show me all the country delights but also give me a mental list of what not to do. These walks probably saved my life in the long run. Gran's sister, Aunt Anne, lived in a part of Mill Cottage with her husband Uncle Albert. They hadn't been able to have children so my brother and I were always welcome in their domain. Aunt and I got on so very well together, she was so easy to talk to that I always made it my business to look for her. Uncle Albert, as well as working in a fish and chip shop in Bath, was also the local river warden. Uncle had been trained by Grandad and had taken over when he died. Apparently they had been a great team, got on well together and thrived on their work. He was a quiet man but had a real sense of humour as I was to find out a bit later.

There was a huge pond around the back of the old decrepit mill. This was originally a reservoir for the water that was used to work the large water wheel when the mill was operational but it was now used to breed trout that were let loose in the local rivers when they were big enough. The pond water was clear and when I got hot and tired during the summer I would sit on the bank watching those trouts' activities. I fell asleep there more than once. Above that large pond were several smaller ones where the tiny trout started off in life until they graduated to the bigger pond. Uncle Albert was not keen on having two small boys rushing around up there because it tended to frighten the fish. Quite by accident that problem was solved one day when I espied two or three odd-looking, long thin creatures in a shallow pond up there. Seeing me transfixed, Uncle told me they were eels and asked if I would like a closer look at them. I was not sure but he pulled one out all the same. I had a really good, close look and it was not only ugly but also a bit menacing. And then it happened. That eel wound itself around Uncle's arm. I was thunderstruck, it looked so powerful. What was Uncle going to do and would it bite? The look on my face must have been a picture for it certainly made Uncle laugh a lot. But the worst was to come. Uncle held out his arm and said 'Here, you can have it if you like'. By then tears of laughter were rolling down his cheeks. All I can remember was beating a hasty retreat. If I was becoming too rowdy up there after that, all Uncle had to do was ask if I would like to handle one of his eels.

Uncle David, Dad's youngest brother, was a different kettle of fish. He was just nine years older than me and I can only describe him as an action man. In those days most people had wood and coal fires so firewood was always in demand. Part of Uncle's farm was used for the production of firewood and Sunday morning was used to get a stock of timber back to the farm. Dad, Uncle Harold and any Uncle that was available went out, cut down trees, burnt the brushwood and hauled the timber over a period of time back home. There was a large circular saw that was used to cut those timber lengths into logs and then they were bagged up. My brother and I were taken along. Our jobs were simple, we kept the brushwood fire going and bagged up wood chips that the axes caused to fly about. The circular saw was a different proposition. We didn't have to be told how dangerous it was. I watched from a distance, terrified that Uncle David might have an accident. When he split the larger chumps with an axe, he made it look so easy. Every time I had a go the axe sunk into the chump and

Carolyn, Julia, Helen and Jean

Carolyn and Julia

Michael, Helen and Gerald

stayed there. Uncle David was a very good footballer, at one time he played for Bath City youth team. To practise at home he had a leather football stuffed with newspapers. Of course my brother and I were keen to join in. Dribbling around the lawn was great fun, being in goal was hair raising. We took it in turns to stand between two of the apple tree trunks and tried to stop Uncle David's best shots. I don't know if giving it some leather would describe it but to us those shots felt like soft cannon balls. Uncle David had to kick that heavy ball quite hard to get it off the ground and we were determined to show no fear in stopping it. The only way was to push our hands out in front and try, not only to slow it down, but also stop it, there was no way that ball was going to bounce off any part of our bodies, that was far too painful. We would go home with the palms of our hands bright red and stinging but we loved every second of it.

Uncle David was quite handy with a shotgun too, he would shoot down pigeons when needed and Gran would cook them for supper. Because they were such a big family and money was extremely short, they had by necessity learned to live off the land; to them it as normal. One of the jobs I was given to help out was to pluck some of the pigeons. It helped stop me becoming squeamish about various aspects of farm work and had its rewards for Gran was a fantastic cook. It was when my brother and I were dribbling Uncle David's heavy football around one day when I stopped for breath and looked up at the house. I happened to glance at an upstairs bedroom window where something held my attention. Looking down at me was a figure of a person wearing a light grey cloak that somehow didn't seem solid and seemed to be smiling at me. I just stood and looked and in a short while he slowly turned away and moved towards the bedroom wall where I lost sight of him. He was so indistinct that he didn't appear to be flesh and blood. I wasn't frightened; it was as if he had been enjoying watching us playing football. I had overheard conversations between the family at odd moments about 'happenings' but we weren't meant to hear, I suspect. Later on in my life I was told that one of Dad's brothers, Uncle Bob, had found it difficult to sleep at nights because he sensed a presence. In the end a priest was brought in to exorcise his room. It seemed to work and the priest said that whatever it was had gone out to the fields outside. I can still picture my apparition in my mind now, though I can't explain who or what it was. As it didn't frighten me I never let it worry me, I just got on enjoying my life down there.

Home life was going well. It was never boring with a younger brother and three even younger sisters. I was never fond of playing dollies but the girls bonded together well. One cannot have too much of a good thing, at least Mum and Dad must have thought not, and along came baby Helen. She automatically became the centre of attention and why not. Despite now having a much more modern house with all mod cons, the size of our family must have been a bit wearing for our parents. To help ease things a routine was observed. The three eldest were drafted into washing and wiping up. A written rota was pinned up inside a cupboard door after fighting broke out as to who did what. It went like this – Michael wash up. Gerald wipe up, Jean put away. After the next mealtime it was Jean to wash up, Michael wipe up, Gerald put away and so on. It helped the washer up to stand on a chair at first. We were happy to be of use. Disagreements and fights would break out occasionally so going outside to play became commonplace. There was always one or more of our friends in the same situation, all was well at the Glebe.

As well as school, my brother and I were now going to Sunday school. We pupils were split into three groups according to age. Mrs Adams, the vicar's wife, took the oldest ones and Miss Ward and Miss Lawrie took the younger ones. I found I understood and enjoyed religion. Undoubtedly it was the way it was taught and explained as we went along that gave us a true understanding of the Bible. It gave for a peaceful and enjoyable hour or two and I always looked forward to it. There was a small organ which was played to give us guidance when we sang a hymn. It was there that I found my singing voice. Eventually I got too old for Sunday school and I, along with two others, were drafted into the church choir.

Chapter 5

A Wild Time

Freshford village now felt like home and as we got older we also got bolder. We had made good friends with other children from the village at school but having the village cut in half gave us a small feeling of isolation. The thing that cut our part of the village from the main part, which included the church and shops, was the Tyning road, field and wood. In olden days there had been a tollgate at our end and the gap had never been closed. To bridge that gap we youngsters would have to travel away from the security of our estate. Tyning Wood became our favourite playground, not just for us younger ones but also for the older boys. There was access to the river and the challenge of going up and down the steep bank. Tree climbing was something I was never ever good at but I kept practising along with the rest.

The older boys had devised a really super game in a certain section of the woods. They had found some large creepers climbing up the trees and cut them off at the base. By taking a creeper end up the steep bank, running down while hanging on tightly to the creeper, their feet would eventually leave the ground and they swung into space. Seeing those lads enjoying themselves so much, pretending to be Tarzan, inspired us to have a go. Unfortunately I drew the short straw, or rather the short creeper. I could only catch hold of mine at full stretch. I did the only thing I could in the circumstances. I went up the bank and ran down at speed and as I passed the creeper I reached up and grabbed it. I immediately knew I had got it wrong. Sure enough as expected, I soared upward and outward and felt as if I was flying in space. Then as I feared, my half a grasp was not enough to keep me on the end of that creeper and I slipped off. I was so far up and going so fast the law of gravity never worked straight away and I soared through the trees. Eventually I hit the ground and slid along on my backside only stopping after sweeping one of the other boys off his feet. I walked home with a sore backside and a pair of ripped trousers but quite relieved that I had missed all the trees on the way down. My parents were not at all happy and told me so. They couldn't afford a new pair of trousers so Mum patched them and told me that patch would act as a reminder not to act so stupidly in the future. I did retire from being Tarzan.

Bad news was around the corner. Bobbie Rose and family were moving away. He was about the same age as Robert and me. Our little team was broken up and things were not the same for a while. His family moved to Southampton and we thought that was it, gone forever. One day a long time after, I was down at Uncle's farm when Robert came up the road. 'There's somebody down on the bridge who would like to see you', he said. Intrigued, I followed him down there and to my surprise there stood Bobbie, dressed and looking immaculate in a Royal Navy uniform. We had a long chat during which he told us that he was a sea cadet and hoped one day to be a fully fledged sailor and travel all over the world. After wishing him well, I went back to the farm expecting to meet up with him again one day. This is sixty three years on and neither Robert nor I have seen him since.

The winters were fun in those days, at least for small boys when it snowed. Snowballing got boring after a while but sledging never did. Freshford is a very hilly place. We soon learnt that sliding out of control can pose a bit of a problem for a small boy on a sledge so we kept mainly to the fields. The best one came down behind Limpley Stoke's St Mary's Church and we were joined by children from the village which was next door to ours. I have a feeling we would start off in Limpley Stoke and finish up in Freshford. The field had a small valley in it; one went down one hill and up the other, across the top and down the side of that one. If we went fast enough we then went over a footpath and took off for a short while, eventually finishing up at the bottom gate covered in snow. My brother and I used a sledge that belonged to Dad's family. It was, and still is, very fast indeed. There is a plaque on the side which says 'The strength of the toy is a joy to the boy'. After a long period of sledging on that field the route down became a sheet of ice; brakes would have come in useful at times like that. If the river flooded before the freeze came along, large pools of water didn't drain back into the river and made wonderful skating rinks.

Our November 5th bonfires were getting better every year. For the first two years Dad was instrumental in the building of our fires. He built a wigwam-like frame which we would cover in bits of fallen branches or any pieces of brushwood we could find in the area. Newspapers, dried leaves, anything that burnt well, would be put inside the wigwam. The guy was put on top and it was lit; it always went well. My friends helped with ours until ambition got the better of them and they decided to build their own. The third year was a taste of what was to come. Every scrap of driftwood, for want of a better word, was piled onto that fire. Someone had the bright idea of going to the local garage and getting two drums of dirty oil that had been drained from car engines and which the garage owner didn't know what to do with. He let us have a couple of old car tyres as well. Everything flammable that could be scrounged from the local households was used. To get the guy on top we needed a ladder. It was a beautiful bonfire; it must have been seen for miles around and villagers came along and joined in the fun. When it died down we put potatoes in the embers but they mostly finished up as cinders. That did it. Next year was to be bigger and better, said the ambitious ones.

Next year came around. Some scrap wood had been found during the year and put by, but because of the way we had cleaned up the immediate area we had to wander further afield and that was hard work. I am afraid we took to cutting small branches off trees and knocking on doors asking for burnables. Eventually we were satisfied. It was a huge bonfire and we would climb up the ladder and sit on top like King Kong. As last year, the drums of dirty oil were brought ready as well as a couple of old car tyres, but we got greedy. The garage owner told us of another garage along the main Warminster road that had plenty of tyres to spare. Half a dozen of the older boys set off. It was about two miles away and sure enough the garage owner was only too glad to let us have them. To get them back we bowled them like hops. It was fun but we were quite tired by the time we arrived at the top of the hill that went down towards the village. We hit on the idea of letting them run down the hill. There was a bank and low stone wall that might stop them. Someone went down first to watch out for traffic and pedestrians and then one by one they were let down that hill. It was quite a sight, every bit as spectacular as we had hoped. A tyre would go down gathering speed as it went, hit the bank or wall, go up high in the air and then bounce to a standstill whereupon the boy below would remove it and the owner come down to retrieve it. Everything went well until mine, which was the last one but it was not my lucky day. Instead of lying down it wobbled slowly around and then disappeared down the road on the right hand side. Realising the danger, I ran as fast as I could to the bottom where the others had just noticed the runaway car tyre. I was horrified and shot off down the road before the others could.

Rosemary Lane is an exceptionally steep and narrow hill and I knew I could be in trouble if I didn't catch my tyre. As fast as I ran he tyre went faster and sped off down that steep hill. To make my fears worse, I heard a motor engine and knew that a disaster was about to happen. I heard a bump, the motor stopped and, then after a wait, carried on. At that moment I became a coward, turned to my left, ran across the field and didn't stop until I got home. I was sat on the steps in the back garden when the others bowled their tyres up to the fire. I went down and told them that mine had gone down into the river and floated away, which in fact I was to find out later that it had. But that is not the end of the story. The motor coming up the hill was my Uncle Harold in his pick-up truck. He could hardly believe his eyes when he saw a lone car tyre coming straight at him at high speed. The lane was too narrow to take avoiding action. He did the only thing possible; he ducked as low as he could. The tyre hit the front of the truck, bounced off the top of the cab and then disappeared down the road behind him. Uncle stopped and looked for damage but there was none so he carried on up the hill hoping to find a culprit. He related this tale to Dad who was also then shocked and angry. The next day Dad noticed he car tyres down by the bonfire and put two and two together. He asked me if I had anything to do with it. I admitted my guilt. After giving me a dressing down (verbally) I was sent to apologise to Uncle. He made the most of the situation and by the time he had finished telling me what a naughty boy I was, in some rather strong language, I felt very small indeed.

Uncle Harold was my godfather and the closest in age to Dad. They both got on so well they never quarrelled. After leaving school Harold went to work in the local flock mill which was a very dirty, dusty job. He soon left and got a job looking after a farmer's chickens. He loved the work so much that he started up on his own and never looked back. He folded it up when the war started, then he served in the navy and was lucky enough to return alive. He restarted his chicken farm and kept going through thick and thin times. It was an extremely difficult life doing everything on his own but his family could see how hard he worked and chipped in their time, helping out when they could.

The bonfire, by the way, became a bit of a disaster. First of all a neighbour noticed that it was too near the telegraph wires and it was too high and liable to topple over when it was well alight. There was a lot of moaning and groaning at first but in the end we moved and lowered it. It looked a shadow of its former self. To make matters worse, when it was lit those car tyres gave off thick black smoke. Everybody on the estate had to shut their doors and windows and those on foot who stood the wrong side of it had to beat a hasty retreat. We were banned for evermore from having another bonfire there.

Life isn't fair sometimes. It wasn't for Mum and Dad, in fact for none of us. Mum, who was expecting her seventh baby, miscarried. I remember that day so well. It happened at home with Dad and Gran Lintern in attendance. The looks of fear and worry were something I have never forgotten. We children stayed quiet downstairs and sensed Dad and Gran's relief when the ambulance came. I went to stay with Gran Lintern at Mill Cottage and my brother stayed with Mum's sister, Aunt Muriel, at first but joined me at Mill Cottage later on. I am not sure where my sisters went but I am sure they were all taken good care of. Mum must have been quite ill as it was a couple of weeks or so before I was taken to visit her at a convalescent home. She was as pleased to see me as I was to see her but she still looked weak and unwell. Gran saw that I got to school on time and saw me home and she also made sure I got to bed on time. Her experience of bringing up her brood meant that looking after me was second nature. Gran had a will of iron but did it all with a smile on her face. She had a rhyme that she used when she saw we were reluctant to go to bed on a bright summer's evening. The first line went: 'Up to bed goes Johnny, grumbling all the way'. The rest I am not sure about. We would sometimes getup again and watch family members who were outside. Aunt may was progressing but her leg had not improved. On a Saturday morning I could hear Gran and Aunt Anne giving Aunt May's leg physiotherapy but the feeling never came back into it. She was fitted with a metal calliper in the end to give her support when she walked. Uncle Fred, the brother next in age to her, also gave her a lot of support morally and physically. He would stay in the evenings and give her good company. He was a brilliant actor and some of those evenings he would learn his lines for the village's next play. Aunt May had also taken part before she got ill, along with Aunt Louise, Uncle Harold's wife.

The Freshford Players were very special. They always played to full houses. It was in the time when televisions were few and far between and those actors and actresses filed a void in people's lives. Comedies were the most popular and most common of the plays put on in the village hall. The children who attended would congregate at the back of the room and sit on the backs of chairs to get a better view. Uncle Fred was very good at comedy. He was a very good actor, full stop, and continued his amateur career until late in life. He did it because he enjoyed it. He was quite talented as an artist and painted the parts of the surrounding countryside that he loved best. Another of Uncle's hobbies was making woollen patterned rugs which looked and felt luxurious. He was lucky not to lose an eye one time when he accidentally caught himself with the tool he used. Uncle Harold's dog Topsy got a lot of affectionate attention when she and Uncle Fred met. Watching them play together made me realise that an animal will respond very well to the right kind of treatment. I never forgot that fact. Uncle also learnt to drive and bought a car. He took me along with Gran, Auntie May and my brother on many trips to interesting places.

One of these jaunts was to Colerne aerodrome about six or seven miles away. It had been used during the war by aircraft, in fact most of them had flown over our heads when I was living with Mum, Gran and Grandad at Westwood. As well as an air display there were war planes of all shapes and sizes on static standing display. People were very keen to get a close look at them and one at least, a large Lancaster bomber, had a long queue waiting patiently to look inside. I joined the queue and entered that large aircraft. I can't remember if any other member of our family went with me. The feeling I had was one of awe, it was a much different world in there. We filed along, slowly taking in all we could see, even sitting in the pilot's seat in the cockpit. All was going well until someone in the pilot's seat decided to move something in the cockpit. It turned out to be the brake and the aircraft moved forward. Panic immediately set in and everybody rushed to get out of the door. By the time I got out, the Lancaster had stopped moving and the ground staff had put chocks under the wheels, something that had been forgotten before. They probably thought noboby would be daft enough to let the brake off. It certainly gave me a thrill that was never matched by other trips to the seaside or elsewhere.

Uncle Fred had a very good friend who emigrated to Canada, in fact they both went. Uncle stayed for many years but eventually returned. Before he went he attempted to give Aunt May driving lessons. She was making a brave effort to get back to normal. She was now up and about and learning to cope with her disability. Auntie enjoyed her lessons but, as she told me years later, if another vehicle came towards her she tended to shut her eyes until it had passed. After deciding she was too nervous, her driving career came to an end.

Chapter 6

Mill Cottage, the farm and countryside

My love affair with Mill Cottage, Uncle's farm and the surrounding countryside really started in a big way when I went to stay at Mill Cottage when Mum became ill. Before, with daily visits, I only got a fleeting glance of the true essence of the place. To start with, because I went to school every day, I was kept to the house area. Saturday morning was great fun. I would go to Bath with Uncle Harold to Evans' fish and chip shop where Uncle Albert worked and bring back food waste. It made a welcome change to the week's routine. Uncle's dog Topsy seemed to enjoy it as well. She couldn't, or wouldn't, sit down in the van and would spend the whole journey standing behind him with her head on his shoulder with her hair being swept back by the wind from the open window. It must have been a bit chilly in the winter. It was good to watch the people passing by while we waited for our cargo to be loaded on board. It was a bit of a shock one day when a tall man in a black overcoat stopped on the other side of the road and leant against the wall. He then, to my shocked amazement, dropped flat on his face and never moved. People were stopping and were trying to help but at that point our time was up and Uncle drove away. The food waste was boiled up in a large boiler fuelled by a wood fire underneath. It needed constant feeding with any dried pieces of fallen wood from the hedges or wood nearby. Those pigs lived quite well on fish and chips and mushy peas which Uncle mixed with a special mill flour.

The school summer holidays came along which meant I had unlimited spare time, or at least I thought I had. What was I going to do with all that spare time? My first inclination was to explore the surrounding countryside. Looking out from the safety of Mill Cottage had whetted my appetite, not to mention being taken on walks by family members. When I was quite small I remember going for a ride up the river near Mill Cottage in the large wooden rowing boat that was kept permanently moored down there. It belonged to the river authorities but was in Uncle Albert's charge as he was the river bailiff. Two large wooden oars were hung up on a garden wall. When they were taken down I got interested. Usually it was for river bailiff work but occasionally the family decided to go on a river trip. I have no idea how many went but that boat seemed pretty full. It was always a happy occasion with plenty of smiles and chatter but all good things come to an end. Whether it became damaged, rotten or leaky I don't know but the boat sank. For years afterwards I watched that sunken boat gradually disappear below the surface of the river. Uncle's next boat, being less sturdy, was quite unable to take a large party so that was the end of it.

The weir on the river was always popular in summer time with villagers and trippers. It seemed like a little piece of heaven for me. Just as one of my Uncles had taken my brother and me down to a shallow area to show us how to catch loggerheads, crayfish and stone loach in jam jars, so Uncle Harold took us down the weir to try to teach us to swim. Being an ex-sailor he was a good swimmer but despite his best efforts we couldn't master the art. The one good thing that it did was show how dangerous that deep water was. It was a lesson well learnt and probably saved our lives more than once. The weir and river were like a magnet to me. I never ceased to enjoy and feel at peace with the world whilst I was there. In fact sixty and more years on, it's still my favourite place to visit.

There was a footbridge consisting of two long thick planks and a handrail that enabled people to get across to the island and the other side of the weir. That footbridge was under trees and the water was clear and fast flowing which attracted a large amount of trout. There were also a lot of gnats and midges flying just above the surface of the water and the trout constantly came to the surface to grab a snack. I spent a long time watching the proceedings until those biting midges drove me away. There was a second weir next to the rubber factory that was accessible from the island but was too dangerous to play on. When I had tired of watching the activities of the trout, kingfishers, moorhens and ducks I would try my luck at fishing out any good looking article that would be going around and around below the weir. Many weird and wonderful things were washed down the river and would be caught up in the whirlpool. It was an irresistible challenge to fish out those objects.

Freshford Weir

The old mill was less attractive to me now I knew that the four upper floors were a no-go area but there were times when it regained its old excitement. In summer when many birds nested in there and hundreds of bats, at least it seemed that many, would come out as it started to get dark and fly all around the area of the huge pond catching many midges that seemed to fill the air. It was an amazing sight. The mill also held one great mystery which I treated with respect and caution. There was a large man-made hole stretching the full width of the ground floor, pitch black in the darkness with the sound of running water coming from down below. I was told later that it was where the now missing huge water wheel had been. I couldn't resist standing on the edge peering into the darkness below. The very large pond at the back of the mill which was used to feed the water wheel in years gone by was now used to breed trout. I was lucky enough to see them being taken out and transported away a couple of times. It started with a team of men from the river authority arriving in a big lorry with a couple of tanks on board filled with water. Next, the pond was emptied by opening the sluice gate allowing the water to flow into the gaping hole in the mill and then off into the river. The trick was for the men in high wading boots to net the fish as the pond level got lower, empty them into buckets of water, which were pulled out by other men using long ropes, and deposit them into the tanks. I always felt a bit sorry for those men, they worked so hard. When the pond was emptied they went round ploughing through deep mud making sure no fish had been missed and left to die in the mud. When all was finished, those men looked exhausted but happy that all had gone well. The fish themselves were distributed into local rivers and the next lot of small fish were introduced to the pond.

Another attraction was a very large hazelnut tree at one end of the pond. I almost developed an addiction to those nuts. The first autumn I really noticed the tree was when Aunt May bravely made her way up there with me in tow, explaining that the nuts could be eaten and showing me how to break them using a stone and a hollow in the garden wall. Some days later she told me the nuts were ready to come down and asked if I would I like some. That afternoon I turned up with a large bag but Aunt was quick to point out she only meant a pocketful. It was an amazing sight to see two large fit uncles shake that tree. Those nuts came down like hailstones. It was great fun picking them up.

The back garden was huge and divided into sections. It was well cultivated and looked after by my Uncles who worked their socks off on their own patch to keep their large family fed. I found feeding dandelion leaves through the wire mesh in front of the rabbit hutches quite rewarding. Those pet rabbits reminded me of the two that we had at Westwood before I let them escape. There were also ferrets though we were warned that they could bite very hard. A young one called Joey was quite affectionate but Uncle Albert's had a bad reputation so I gave him a wide berth. My brother and I were taken out one Sunday morning to a quiet part of the countryside along with the ferrets. They were put down rabbit holes to drive them out, which they did. We were making a little too much noise apparently so we were requested to stand nearby holding the dead rabbits. It was a morning I didn't enjoy and told Gran this. Fortunately the experience wasn't repeated.

The front of Mill Cottage consisted of a lawn, flower beds and apple trees but there was one area that was cultivated. In that place there used to be a deep well. Sadly the family's dog, Bob, fell down there and died so it was filled in, mostly with household waste. Friary Wood was next to the house and farm. It was somewhere I could wander in at will. The natural delights and discoveries were endless. I tended to go missing for a long time. One of the things I tried my hardest at was tree climbing. I had found out to my cost and embarrassment on first arriving in the village that I was not good at it. There was a natural competitiveness in the games we played getting to know the other local children but I had never climbed a tree before the time we converged on an old, thick but fairly short, tree at the bottom of the estate. It looked as if it would be possible for all of us to get to the top of the main trunk at the same time so that was what we tried. Those less able were helped up by the better climbers. We stayed up there, shouting out to any passing car, cyclist or pedestrian on the lane below, feeling like decorations on a Christmas tree. Time went by and we tired of that game so we started back down. I suddenly realised I found it harder to go down and lost my nerve. The others found that funny and despite my asking for help, they disappeared down the lane laughing all the way. Still frightened and not knowing what to do, I just stayed there feeling more miserable by the minute. After what seemed an age, an old lady came by. It must have been the look on my face that made her ask what was I doing up there. After telling her what a rotten lot of so and sos my so called friends had done, she gently and carefully guided me down. That lady and I became good friends.

My aim in Friary Wood was to climb to the top of the huge beech tree that had names carved into it. I tried on my own, and sometimes with others, to get to the top of the tree and carve my name into its bark. I only ever got three quarters of the way up, the last part was extremely difficult. It was the bigger, taller boys who accomplished it. By the time I grew to that size I had decided that what I had achieved as a youngster was satisfying enough. The tree was a beautiful thing, not only was it a village landmark, its large umbrella of branches seemed to stop other trees or brambles from growing beneath. In the Spring its fresh green leaves were a picture; in the Autumn beech nuts fell and I enjoyed them along with the birds, then it was the turn of the golden brown leaves to fall, forming a fantastic carpet. Memories are made of this sort of beauty. For a period of time, two robins who had built their nest under a root of the tree, laid eggs and brought up a family. I spent a lot of time watching that nest until the young had flown. I'm ashamed to admit I took one egg out of a nest. After checking there was not chick inside, I made a hole in each end with a pin and then blew the insides out, taking care to handle the egg gently. I thought I was so clever until Mum pointed out it was not a nice thing to do so and I ended that hobby. I took to just finding nests and watching the infants grow up until they flew. I came across my first and only cuckoo in that way. It involved a blackbird's nest. I didn't realise what was happening at first but after telling the family of the unusual happenings, I saw the two parent blackbirds feed the young trespasser until it grew bigger than them and flew off. One Saturday Uncle Albert took me for a ride up the river in his boat. On Sunday morning I had fried moorhen eggs for breakfast but it only happened once.

I enjoyed walking, sitting and listening in that wood. Nature was my new love. I spent so much time doing my own thing my absences began to worry the family so Uncle Harold started to find me small chores around his farm to keep me from wandering off. They were tasks that I got to enjoy. I felt I was being useful and a proper family member. Uncle Harold was married to Louise with a young son David, followed later by a daughter Ann. They lived in a cottage in a small hamlet called Friary. The connecting dirt road between Friary and the farm and Mill Cottage was referred to as the track. Uncle's was a seven day a week job. He let his chickens outside into fields surround by wire mesh. They were lucky to enjoy such a long active life in that environment but there was a snag. The local foxes also noted those fine healthy chickens and constant vigilance was needed to keep them out.

Hen houses

They weren't called cunning for nothing so we tried not to give those foxes any chance. One of the chores I had was to go around pulling up the high wire fences until I found some slackness or attempted entry. I would hammer a pointed wooden peg with a nail stuck into the side to hold the wire tight or re-attach it into the soil. I also took part in egg collecting I took part in but Uncle did the feeding. Mucking out was a necessary evil. The chicken poo had a strong smell of ammonia but I never got to dislike it. The heavy, hard job was cleaning out the water bowls and carrying buckets of water along the track to fill them up. As there were five houses with fields in between, my gallivanting off to the river, weir and woods became less frequent. To be honest, I was more likely to be found lying down somewhere.

The farm cats were a constant source of interest and intrigue. They were nervous and elusive, almost wild in fact. Uncle would put food down for them and he was the one they came close to. After he told me nobody else could get anywhere near them, I decided to prove him wrong. He told me which one of the four was the most anti-social and that one was my goal. It took a long, long time to gain its confidence and even longer to touch it. I was surprised the day I picked it up for the first time it was so easy. The sardine sandwich I had in my hand may have had something to do with it. Uncle wasn't prepared for the change and on seeing me approach the cat, he warned me to keep away because it would scratch my hand off. His face was a mixture of shock and disbelief when I picked it up and walked towards him. That moment of triumph went to my head. Every animal and bird I came across after that had to be my tame friend but it didn't always work out that way. One day I overheard somebody say to Gran, 'Michael's just gone up the wood to charm the birds out of the trees.' One lot of birds that I found fascinating was a glass domed display case containing stuffed foreign birds. They were in Aunt Ann's living room but actually belonged to Gran. Aunt Ann always made me welcome, I found her easy to get on with and we would both chatter away.

My attempts to make friends with Uncle's pigs were successful because they loved being scratched and would stick their wet noses above the sty to get more. We were warned not to venture in with them especially one huge breeding sow that allowed only Uncle into her domain. I saw more than one very hurried exit from her sty by other family members. Those small piglets were so cute when born but woe betide anybody who picked one up. The moment their feet left the ground they let out a loud squeal which then brought a charging mother to the rescue. There was one snag about those sties. In the base of one of the walls were holes and a container let into the ground on the outside with holes in the sides. This was to take the water and muck that accumulated when the sties were brushed and washed out. Water took a long time to seep away so those containers usually had some, if not a lot, of extremely smelly liquid in them. It always came as a shock to anybody who forgot they were there. To my embarrassment I filled my wellington boots up more than once but at least it gave everybody else a good laugh.

On a few occasions I took some of my friends down to the farm. On one of those visits Stephen stepped into the pig's waste container. We actually felt a bit sorry for him on his half mile walk home. I bet his parents were not amused either. All my friends came one memorable Saturday morning, the day allotted for the trip into Bath for the pig swill food. On looking at the half dozen of us standing at the back of his van Uncle told us, 'You can't all get in there, there's not enough room, okay'. He then turned around and got in the driving seat. To his astonishment the van was full of small boys who had interpreted the last word, 'okay', as meaning that he had changed his mind. Uncle, who saw the joke, said nothing more at that stage and drove us there and back without mishap. We all agreed it was a great experience despite getting a bit grubby from the waste food bins. This sort of visit decreased over time my friends satisfied their curiosity about what I got up to down on the farm and, as I had my usual jobs to do around the place, time was limited.

I had graduated to being in charge of the wood fire under the boiler that held the pig swill. I was warned not to let the fire go out or I would be for it. I never questioned what Uncle said because I enjoyed keeping that fire going. Fire had a fascination for me. The wood used was dried and dead pieces from around the farm, inside the old mill and, best of all, from the wood next door. This meant that I was up the wood on legal business. I took the opportunity with both hands to do my own thing as well. The boiler fire had a door on it, just like a miniature furnace with a space underneath for the ashes to drop. In later years when I had graduated to senior school and pottery was on the agenda, in a moment of inspiration, I waded into the middle of the nearby river and dug some blue clay out of the bottom of it. I fashioned a bowl and quite a nice egg cup out of the clay and put both under the boiler's fire until they set and hardened. I was so proud and delighted with my achievements when I presented them to the teacher during my next lesson. To my horror she crushed my beautiful little egg cup as she explained that they were cottage industry projects, not as good and strong as commercial china one buys in the shops. She then seemed to remember me, looked me full in the face and said, 'Did you mind me doing that?' As it was now too late anyway and I didn't want to lose face in front of the class, I just mumbled, 'no', after getting over the shock. More than sixty years later I am still the proud owner of the bowl.

Boiler

Other routine jobs included washing the poo off chicken's eggs; it was a bit of an art as none were to be dropped or damaged. Feeding the hens and collecting the eggs now and then was a bit of a treat -until I came across a hen that had gone broody. If I tried to take the egg or eggs out, she would lay into my hand with her beak, defending her chosen eggs at all cost. I found it a painful experience until I decided to hold the hen's head down before venturing underneath. Uncle would put those hens in a cage on their own with a china egg in the nestbox. After trying to hatch them without success, they seemed to give up and return to normal. Despite our persistent efforts, every now and again a fox would get among the chickens and cause havoc. They didn't just kill one for food; they killed every one they could catch. It was heartbreaking for Uncle, working on a shoestring and barely making ends meet. On one occasion the fox got in through the floor slats, killed the whole lot in that large house and then found it couldn't get out again. On discovering this tragedy next morning Uncle shot the fox. It didn't make us feel any better because his loss was so great. On another occasion the carnage was less bad, most of the hens got away except for two who had leg and wing breakages. My brother had joined me at Mill Cottage as the school holidays had come to an end and we were back at the village school again. Gerald and I watched as Uncle painstakingly put wooden splints on the breaks and held them in place with bandages. He put the hens inside a special run in the old building next to the mill that served as his base and storage area. My brother and I were then put in charge of those injured chickens. We fed and watered them before we went to school and when we came back. We petted them as though they were our pet cats or dogs and they responded in like manner. Uncle said they would become quite active just before we turned up. They always ran to greet us and I loved them to bits. We were doubly proud of them as the still laid eggs. Came the day when Uncle took off their bandages and splints and put them back in the pen. It was great to see their wounds were healed. A few days later on, coming home from school, the hens were missing. According to Uncle they had gone to market. All we could do was accept it and hope they had gone to a new home. Uncle had an incubator. With new chicks being born and growing up, the older hens would sometimes have to move on to other farms, like it or not. Farms were always on the move.

One day two of my Uncles, Harold and David, decided to have a bit of fun at my brother's and my expense. A group of young pigs were getting too big for the sty so they were going to have to leave home and Mum and go into more roomy quarters. The chaos, confusion and the anger of Mum who was locked inside the house, meant everything had to be done quickly. The best way was to catch the youngsters one by one, put them in hessian sacks, tie the necks and hand them to someone outside the sty. It looked easy enough until I was ushered into the pen. My first job was to catch a piglet. I would catch one but, as soon as I tried to pick it up to put into my sack, it would let out a very loud squeal. This would stir the others up who would then tear around bumping into me and knocking me over onto the very mucky floor. On losing my grip I would have to start again. Those piglets were not only heavy, they were putting up a good fight. After several efforts I had not only failed to get a single piglet into a sack but my Uncles were laughing themselves silly. As Mum was getting very angry and was trying to batter the interior door down the uncles took over from me, much to my relief. They caught the piglets, put them into sacks and handed them over the wall to us two boys. That's when our troubles really started. On putting those sacks on the ground, there would be a period of quiet stillness and then the sacks would take off at high speed. There were about ten or twelve of them, I can't remember exactly how many. Although the piglets couldn't see where they were going, they just ran everywhere. There was a large pond at one end, a fifteen foot drop into the old mill at one side and the doorway and a flight of stairs inside Uncle's storage building at the other. Those rampaging idiots in sacks seemed determined to escape. It was one of the most tiring experiences of my life! Eventually the Uncles joined us and carried them to their new sty, leaving two very mucky and tired boys to find a resting place.

The sequel to this came a couple of weeks later. Every time I passed the sty and looked at the lone mum, she would look up at me. There was no way I could tell what she was thinking or how she had taken her loss. She could no doubt hear her piglets making hay in their new home. I was to find out one day when I stopped and leant over the wall and spoke to her. She walked up to me with her snout in the air and made grunting noises. On reaching over to her I accidentally knocked the large stiff-bristled broom, that had been left on the top of the wall, into the sty. My first reaction was to go in and get it but my memory went back to my experiences of trying to catch and lift her young and I then realised I would be no match in a tug of war with that lady. She picked the broom up, carried it to the other end of the sty and proceeded to bite great chunks out of it. Pigs don't look fierce but her jaws were very strong, as I soon came to realise that afternoon. She gradually took that broom to pieces until all that remained were bits of wood and bristles all over her sty. Uncle was out on business at the time. I thought when he came back I might be in trouble but, to my surprise, he praised me for having the good sense to stay outside and not put myself in danger.

Uncle Bob was Uncle Harold's brother, a couple of years younger than him. He, like Uncle Harold, had served in the navy during the war and on his return home found his vocation in the building trade, working for a firm based in the village. His main trade was plumbing but he seemed to be able to turn his hand to anything. This became apparent when he assisted with various repairs, renovations and building projects to help with the smooth running of the farm. He was a cheerful, happy-go-lucky character, the place was always buzzing when he was around. He swept Mill Cottage's chimneys when the need arose. He told me that if the brush became stuck at the top, as it had the bad habit of doing, he would take drastic measures. This entailed going up the rickety stairs inside the mill, going out of the second storey window onto the ridge of the Mill Cottage's roof and making his way along to the chimney stack to free the brush. It was Uncle's sheer attitude to life that inspired me when I also joined the building trade later on. It helped me to see the possibilities in life and even if problems are not easy to solve, there is always an answer.

A case in point was when Uncle purchased a new animal at Trowbridge market. A day out at Trowbridge market was a really special treat. I was only able to go during the school holidays but it had everything that was good about country life. There were animals aplenty being brought in and then leaving after being sold at the auction. Gran liked to take us around the cages that held pet rabbits and guinea pigs, sometimes buying one to join the others in Mill Cottage garden. It all gave me a wonderful experience of what farming was all about. A bit of a mistake was made when the family purchased a large white goat. It looked a good deal at the time. I heard when it was going to be delivered and made sure I was there at the time. The family already had several goats and were aware of their sometimes unpredictable nature. The new goat was unloaded and tied to a ring in the wall at the end of a long rope. After the delivery lorry had gone, someone approached that beautiful white goat and was well and truly butted; so was everybody else who got too near. Food and water were tried but nothing seemed to work. In the hope that a good night's sleep might help, bedding was put down and everybody departed. The next morning Mr Goat remained aggressive so, reluctantly, the previous owner was called to come and take it away. Was the goat upset at being in a strange place or was it just bad tempered?

A much more successful purchase was a brown calf, which was given the name Sally. She was kept in an outdoor enclosure until she grew big and strong enough to be let out into the fields. Other than at the market it was the nearest I had come a young calf. Being in an enclosure on her own, Sally welcomed company and my brother and I spent a lot of time with her. We were still going to school whilst living at Mill Cottage. We said goodbye to Sally in the morning and visited her when we got home. We were late home one day so she jumped out of her stall. She was so friendly that after a while it was like greeting a pet dog.

Eventually Mum returned home and after making sure she could cope with her big family again, my brother and I returned as well. It was great to be back amongst friends and equally good to be back with family. It seemed a bit strange at first and quite cramped after the freedom of Mill Cottage, Uncle's farm and the surrounding countryside. Dad made a point that we were to help Mum whenever she asked for assistance. Not wishing for another family split up, we abided by those rules. My sisters formed into a happy band of girls. Not being entirely happy at playing dollies, I tended to either play or scrap with my brother, or escape from the house. Seeing that I had grown too big for my tricycle Grandad Taylor had lovingly built a two wheeler bicycle in his Westwood workshop. With his engineering skills he had combined left-over parts with some new components and then finished it in cream with red trim. I christened my bike 'Strawberry and Cream' and referred to it as an 'A.S.P.' model, short for 'All Spare Parts'. I loved it to bits. The only trouble was I couldn't ride it. Several of the Glebe gang were in the same boat. We spent hours practising on each other's machines but I failed to progress. Jean Clift, Philip's sister next door, was going out to work travelling backwards and forwards on her bicycle. I became fascinated at the way she came home. She would come shooting down the footpath towards her house and just before she got there, she would jump off. I was never sure whether her brakes didn't work properly or it was an act of bravado. Eventually I plucked up the courage to ask her to teach me to ride. Thankfully she agreed. Jean was quite firm but at the same time encouraging. After many falls and grazes, I actually found I had left Jean behind and was sailing along unaided. That red letter day in my life made me think I had the freedom of the road but my parents I warned me to stay on the estate for the time being. A couple of others who had now mastered the art of cycling went along with me in trying to go one step further. Not content with tearing around the footpaths, we tried to outdo one another with difficult tricks. We thought we were clever, standing on the saddle or riding side saddle while pedalling with one foot, until Philipp, one of the older boys who had helped us newcomers to bond , spotted us and came up to show us his own trick. With a bit of a smile on his face, he sat on the handlebars facing the saddle and pedalled backwards. It worked for him. Of course we all tried it only to find found it was not so easy as it looked. After a lot of bruised shins and total collapses we had to admit we were far from perfect.

Eventually we were let out of the estate and found Freshford village had a lot to offer. With so many hills the most obvious competition was seeing who could get up one of the steep hills without stopping. Rosemary Hill was the steepest. Tyning Wood footpath was a very exciting ride, going down. Anybody having the misfortune to go over the edge would find themselves hurtling down the steep bank towards the river. The river tended to flood during the winter. During heavy flooding it could cover one of the roads down in the valley making it impassable to cars, though pedestrians could walk along the metal railings at the side of the road. One winter our greatest challenge was to see who could progress furthest along the railings by pedalling hard into the flood water. After a few attempts I believed I could win so, starting a long way back, I rode at full speed, surging into the floodwater and making a huge wave on each side. To my delight I got as far as the gate which was the furthest so far, despite the water slowing me a lot quicker than expected. To steady myself I reached out and grabbed the gate only to find it wasn't shut properly. I got very wet that day. The only consolation was that it gave my friends a good laugh.

One of my missions in life was looking for mushrooms when the right time of year came. During my stay at Mill Cottage I had heard the family discussing their finds in the surrounding fields especially in the field next to the weir, so I decided to try my luck. After tramping around the fields during the day a couple of times and finding nothing, I brought my frustration up at a family lunch break. All I got in reply was: 'Maybe someone got up earlier in the morning and beat you to it.' The challenge was set; I had to beat that someone to it. Very, very early one morning I got up to have a go but getting out of the house undetected proved to be the hard bit. My brother and I were in a back bedroom up on the second floor. I crawled on my hands and knees past the bedroom where Uncle David and Uncle Fred were sleeping, the elm floorboards were bare so I had to go very slowly. Next there was the top flight of stairs to get down and then past Aunt May and Gran's bedroom, done without a squeak. The lower stairs were not too difficult, so after putting on my hat, coat and shoes I unlocked the door and set out on my quest. I was out there a long time, it was cold, the grass was wet and, worst of all, I didn't find one mushroom. I managed to get back as quickly as I had left and went back to bed. At lunch break later I confessed what I had done and asked where all the mushrooms had gone. Nobody believed me at first until I showed them my soaking wet shoes. Their general reaction was to tell me please not to do it again and tut about what I was going to do next. Not one word regarding the missing mushrooms. I did find some fruitful areas around the village fields but my quest came to a surprising end one day when I found a huge specimen in one of Uncle's fields. I was told it was a horse mushroom. Mum cooked it and I ate the whole thing in one go. It was delicious but made me heartily sick afterwards, so much so that I couldn't keep a field mushroom down for the next thirty years. Fortunately I can now.

Sally, my pet calf, had now been let out into a field but I was to leave her quiet until she got used to it. There were walnut trees in a little wood next to Uncle's chicken run fields. They were huge yet I never seemed to be able to find many nuts come autumn. The explanation was that squirrels loved them and it was a case of first come, first served. Luckily I found my compensation in the couple or so trees hanging over the Mill Cottage garden wall. The owners next door couldn't have had much of a harvest because I for one made a habit of filling my pockets. I did and still do love walnuts.

The garden was a huge area situated above and to one end of the large mill pond. Some of it was divided into sections and the Uncles worked very hard at it. There was plenty of manure on the farm and water in the pond. It was a treat to see rows of produce, cabbage patches and fruit trees. It taught me that with hard work and dedication gardening could have its own rewards. In the autumn the fruit trees, gooseberry bushes, currant bushes and nut trees received regular visits but I was warned off the strawberry patch and especially banned from Uncle Albert's raspberries. It was also fun to feed the pet rabbits dandelion leaves through the wire mesh at the front of their cages and shoo any marauding herons away, who had come to fish young trout out of the pond. Every now and again when pigeons were shot for the pot, I would be called upon to pluck them. One of the hard facts of life is to learn that animals and birds from both farm and countryside had to be killed and eaten. Plucking those pigeons was the family's way of making me aware of that fact without too much trauma. There is no doubt that the freedom I had to explore the river, weir, Friary Woods, Uncle's farm and Mill Cottage was something that few other youngsters would be so lucky to experience now or even then. Along with the love and care shown to me by my family there, I also picked up such a lot of practical knowledge. I didn't realise at the time just how privileged I was.

Home and village life curtailed the time I spent down at Mill Cottage but Saturdays were always a must. On going home up the steep field I would stop and look down at the old mill, pond and cottage below. The large factory chimney rising out of the mill was such a majestic feature I remained in awe of it. One Saturday morning a rather silly plan entered my head. The metal doors of the fire place at the base of the chimney had disappeared many moons ago. There was only a large hole left there. During the nesting season, crow, rooks and jackdaws made their homes in the large amount of ivy on the outside of the chimney and some would nest inside the top. The air would be filled with their calls then but by now they had all hatched and flown. I wondered what the fireplace would look like if I started up a small fire in there and some smoke came out of the top of the stack. Of course the next step was to find out. With my skills as a firemaker, starting a fire was easy, using some of the fallen birds' nest twigs to set it. My intention was only to have a small fire, watch the smoke come out of the top and then put it out. It was a huge mistake striking that match. All went well to start with but circumstances took over. The fire I had made was on top of a lot of other fallen twigs which also caught light. There was soon quite a blaze going and disappearing up the chimney. All of a sudden, I heard a roaring sound which got louder and louder. There must have been twigs and ivy all the way up inside and the draught coming into the fireplace just fanned the flames. My brother and I knew then that all was lost and nature would have to take its course. An even bigger shock came when we heard Gran calling us for the mid-day break time. We hadn't heard her bugle call and she was now looking for us in person. I suppose we should have run away from the chimney in the hope she wouldn't see it but she was too quick for us. The only solution I had was to stand in front of the opening and try to make myself as big as I could, which wasn't very big in those days.

Gran must have seen and heard that roaring blaze but to my surprise she never uttered a word about the fire behind me. She just turned and walked away and we followed her back down to the house and lunch break. Not only did Gran not mention what she had seen at all that day, neither did my Uncles. I can only guess it was discussed and they decided that, as the mill was not going to burn down, they would leave it to my conscience. That night as we went home, the smoke was still puffing merrily away out of the top of the stack. My thoughts were, 'maybe Gran is keeping quiet; hopefully the smoke will have stopped by the morning and I will be safe from punishment.' But no, the smoke was still coming out next morning. I thought I would be in trouble for sure. My folly was not mentioned that day or the next, in fact not a word of reproach was ever uttered by anyone. If they thought my conscience would prick harder than any words from them, they were right. I was a good boy for a long time after.

Chapter 7

Village Life

Around this time Queen Elizabeth II's coronation took place. Mr Adams, our village vicar, whom I knew well from my time in the choir, came to our school when King George VI died and personally told all the children of the sad news while we were in class. It was typical of him, a caring man who believed in doing the right thing. We choirboys also knew that he had a sense of humour. After King George's state funeral, the new Queen's coronation was held and the parish council decided it was to be a very special day in the life of the village. Not many, if any, working class people had televisions in those days so a television was set up in the village hall. Children were allowed to come and view the coronation, free of charge, in black and white. A lot of children turned up. It started the day off well.

In the afternoon a carnival procession was held. The people of the village were a revelation. Those normally honest, upright, hard working citizens just let themselves go. In fancy dress on the carnival floats they did their best and succeeded to put a smile on everybody's face. Having too much to drink inspired one man to try and carry off the carnival princess. I suppose he could almost be excused as he was dressed up as a pirate. After the parade a fancy dress competition was held for different age classes. In my class, I came second as a paper boy selling papers in the street. Brother Gerald won first prize as a black and white minstrel. We had been made up at Mill Cottage by Uncle Fred, Aunt Louise, Aunt May and Gran. It was a great fun occasion but the excitement became too much for sister Jean and she fainted. I shall never forget it; she went down like a felled tree, landing on the bare boards. It was a miracle she never broke anything. After making sure all was well with her, the show went on.

Before all these proceedings the parish council held an official opening ceremony on the new playing field which had been specially constructed behind the village hall. It had swings, a seesaw and a large slide, a perfect place for the village children. The announcement to the nation that morning that Edmund Hillary and Sherpa Tensing had been the first people to climb Mount Everest just seemed to add to what was a uniquely special day.

After the carnival floats and fancy dress competition the chance came for the boys of the village to let off steam in a running race. To make it fair, the oldest started from the hall and the others started in age groups further up the road. The route for the race was a large loop around the village roads. It was about two miles in distance but seemed much longer by the time we had finished. I, and four or five others, were nearly the front group so we thought we had plenty of space between ourselves and the big boys which gave us confidence. We set off when the shout came back down the road for us to start. Our laughing and joking came to a stop when we heard the unmistakeable sound of the big boys coming towards us in the distance. It then became a case of heads down and run as hard as we could. After another half mile the sound of those big feet came thundering up behind us and those large lads swept us by. We became also-rans, at least all except one of us. To our amazement one of our number, Michael P.W., just sped up and disappeared down the road with the big boys. Those of us he had left behind, too out of puff to speak, looked at each other as if to say, 'Where the hell did he get that from?' Now the race was between those of us that remained. Robert, Royston and I were equally matched and no matter how hard we tried, couldn't shake the others off. As the finishing line at the hall approached with most of the village cheering us on, it became a matter of life or death. Three desperate, exhausted boys threw themselves over the finishing line. I can't remember who came first or second only that I was third. Michael's explanation for his sudden surge and disappearance up the road was that he did cross country running at school. Our day's celebrations were at an end but the adults carried on enjoying themselves in their own way. If people of the world got together on a regular basis as our village did on that day, the world might be a happier place.

Unity and peace were things I experienced and enjoyed after joining St Peter's church choir. The Reverend Adams was the perfect man for the job. He not only had the knack of keeping us younger choirboys in good order but his pleasant, sincere manner made us show due respect to him and religion. I found that I had a good soprano singing voice and, as is so often the case, being good at something makes one enjoy doing it all the more. Thanks were also due to the ladies in the pew behind me. It helped to have their voices coming at me from the rear so that I could mingle in and give it full throttle. Also, any mistakes I made, like forgetting the right note or singing high when I should have been singing low, would be covered by Miss Duck and Muriel's wonderful renditions. They in turn both agreed that their contributions went much better when we boys got it right. Royston, Martin and I were the three older boys. Royston's brother Gerald, my brother Gerald and Alan joined us at a later stage. Facing us on the other side of the aisle were Mr Nobles, Mr Case and Peter whose deep voices contrasted with ours. A shake of the head or a wince would occur from those three stalwarts if we boys sang out of tune or worse, so choir practice was a must. Although I tried, I never could learn to read music but after a bit of intense training I got a rough idea of what those written notes were meant to sound like. What really came to my rescue was the fact that after singing a hymn for the first time, my memory never forgot it; what a bonus.

For a period of time a choir master and music teacher from one of the churches in the nearby town of Bradford-on-Avon joined us in our weekly choir practice. He lived in the village and was a very pleasant and patient man with a huge knowledge of music. I found out later that he had previously been the church organist. Mr Hathaway was very precise; he made us think about the words we were singing, where we needed to sing loud or soft. Singing in tune came naturally after that. We could spend all evening just practising one hymn. The effect of that on Sunday was sometimes dramatic and our confidence soared. Mr Hathaway said that after his training I had a really good voice and he would like to record it though circumstances prevented that from happening. Although everything was in good order, we were still young boys and the odd bit of mischief took place. Thankfully Reverend Adams understood us and his sense of humour helped to calm any situation. There was one Sunday evening, however, when I went too far. We were meant to enter the vestry by walking through the church interior. There was a door in the vestry that was used by anybody who happened to be late. That Sunday evening I decided to have a bit of fun. I walked around to the back of the church until I saw the others through the vestry window. What a good idea, I thought, to rush in through the door making a lot of noise and making them jump with fright. I caught hold of the handle of the door, opened it and rushed in. To my horror it was me that got the shock. I not only entered pitch black darkness but the floor was not there. I dropped downwards, hardly touching the flight of stairs, collided with a wall, went down another flight of stairs and finished up on a lumpy pile. I lay there for a while, well and truly terrified until I heard voices at the top of the stairs. A light was switched on and all things became clear. I was lying on a pile of coal next to the furnace that heated the church. It seemed that I had opened the door on the wrong side of the vestry window and gone down into the furnace room. What a chump. I didn't seem to have broken anything and sustained only a few bruises, so after a good brush down, I took part in Evensong, trying to get over my shock as I did. I played down the incident when I got home, not wanting to be a worry to Mum and Dad. The next day Mr Adams turned up at school and spoke to me personally whereupon I assured him I was suffering no ill effects. I settled down to a more quiet and peaceful existence at church after that.

I loved the hymn 'The day thou gavest Lord has ended' that was used to finish Evensong and I would stay behind to hear Miss Chapman the organist playing away on her own. I never knew, or cared if she knew, that there was only two of us left in the church, it just felt right for me. It came as a huge shock to me and all of us one Sunday morning when somebody came into the vestry and told us that the Reverend Adams had died in the night. A stand-in was found. Reverend Roberts was brought out of retirement from where he lived in the nearby village of Hinton Charterhouse. He fitted in well with all of us, also having a good sense of humour. He was so good with his sermons that I really looked forward to them every week. All good things come to an end, he departed when the Reverend Pollard was brought in as a replacement. He was a good man with the care of his flock uppermost in his mind. He let the newly formed football team use the vicarage as a changing room and started the Sea Scouts. Unfortunately I blotted my copybook by being a bit silly. Mr Pollard's sermons were not so riveting as Mr Roberts' so we found we were marking time while the church service continued on. Someone had the not-too-bright idea of putting his penny underneath his white surplus and wetting it with his finger. The result was that the imprint of the penny was left on the surplice. Within a short while we all had one or two imprints. This quite rightly didn't go down well with Mr Pollard and he made us tell our parents that they were going to have to clean our surplices. Having six children, mum was not amused and told me to inform Mr Pollard that there was no way she going to do that. I told him this and was then asked to leave the choir.

I would recommend living in a village to anyone; it is so different to any other existence if modern transport and cars are left out of the equation. In my young days, the sheer peace and quiet made life more bearable. With fewer people one got to know most of them. Smiles and cheery words were the norm when people passed each other in the street. Gossip was common and everybody kept up with everybody else's business. One soon got to know who were the good guys or the bad guys. In a small village news travels fast, as demonstrated by the time a fruit and veg lorry overturned on a sharp bend of the main Warminster road, on the outskirts of the village. One of the village boys came across the scene shortly afterwards. The driver, who had escaped unharmed, told the boy that some of the goods were too damaged to be sold by his firm so the boy gathered up what he could carry on his bike. On seeing him, and hearing that there might be something going free, a group of young boys were soon off up the road in anticipation. We weren't the only ones; people seemed to arrive from all different directions. By the time I got there the driver was standing guard along with a policeman. The thing that drove people to turn up that day was the fact that food was still on ration and money was in short supply. The driver was good enough to give the youngsters an apple or orange each. Small happenings such as this came and went and life carried on. The coronation celebrations were memorable enough until something much bigger came to town, in a manner of speaking.

Ealing studios came to the area in 1952 to use the beautiful countryside we were so privileged to live in to shoot scenes for the film The Titfield Thunderbolt. The film's plot centred around the efforts of Titfield trying to keep its railway station open against all the odds. Our village was used, along with many others in the area, and the end product, a brilliant comedy film featuring some outstanding actors and actresses, was a classic. Extras for the film were taken from the village communities and ours was no exception. The Freshford village play actors were of course used freely. Uncle Fred and Aunt Louise were two of them and Gran was not forgotten. She would tell Aunt May she had washed up the breakfast things and she was off to work now. Gran featured in one of the opening scenes walking up a hill with others. As I was still in the choir at that time and St Peter's church was used in the film, I and my fellow choristers were welcomed on the set. Although I only spent a week on filming duty it was one of the most memorable ones of my life. It was an extremely busy week. Filming for different scenes was going on constantly, except for one day when it rained. To my utter disappointment the scene of us choirboys walking at speed through the churchyard in our surplices and cassocks was not used in the film. We had the consolation of seeing two scenes of children running after a lorry which in the back had stuffed models rather than real people with us screaming our heads off included. It almost made me feel like a film star.

The one bright part of the week was spending a lot of time with Julian Holloway, the son of Stanley Holloway, one of the main characters and one of Britain's greatest comedy actors. Julian was my age. We got on well and he even joined me at dinner breaks, sharing my cheese sandwiches instead of sitting in his Mum and Dad's Rolls Royce. That's what I call friendship. He also took time to introduce me to some of the actors and explained the procedures of filming. I was only on the set for a week but so much action was packed into that time. To me the film world was amazing and it opened my eyes to the fact that there are other worlds out there. At the end of the week I had to say goodbye to Julian, the film company was moving on to another location and I would have to go back to school. We spent a long time on that last day discussing what we would like to do with our lives, at the same time guessing what the future held. For me life went on as normal, enjoying the good things and getting through the bad times with that great week stamped on my mind giving me added impetus. For Julian I am very glad to say his dreams came true. He told me that he would like to be an accomplished actor, just like his Dad. He sure did. Not only did he appear in serious plays but also in the 'Carry On' films which I watched in the cinema and on television with a smile on my face and with a warm feeling inside which seemed to say, 'well done that man'. I would like to meet him again one day to tell him that personally. The real beauty is that I have the video film of Titfield Thunderbolt and any time the urge takes me, I can go back to those few golden days, as well as seeing myself in short trousers.

Time marches on as I was finding out. I was fully aware that I was approaching the age of eleven when the time would come to leave Freshford's junior and infant school and progress to senior school. I was quite honestly filled with trepidation. Before this happened all of our family went down with chickenpox. It was so difficult to cope, not only did we all feel very ill, we were aware that the normal day to day routine became very hit and miss. Somehow we all survived but its an experience I never want to go through again. The youngest of our brood, Helen, was growing up fast with her three sisters as her protectors and best friends. On one occasion Mum happened to look out of the living room window just as toddler Helen went shooting by on my tricycle. The sheer speed instantly alerted Mum to the possible danger and she reacted immediately. Helen was too small to pedal properly and was pushed around by her older sisters who at that time were watching her enjoy the trip. Mum ran through the house like an Olympian athlete, up through the passageway between our and next door's house and arrived just in time to stop Helen come tumbling down the concrete steps and hurt herself badly. Mum had realised that Helen had only a little control and as expected had gone up the steep path just past our house. From there the only place was down. She was a lucky little girl that day and Mum's quickness saved from serious harm.

My quick thinking saved me and a few friends when we were caught taking walnuts from beneath a tree in a farmer's field. The farmer was leading us back to his farm to, as he put it, 'Meet the law' when I suddenly remembered that his daughter was my classmate at school. In a moment of inspiration, I said that Susan had said we could have some of those walnuts. The farmer stopped in his tracks and after a period of thought he let us go with a warning. We ran away and never went there again. It was around this time that I discovered something was wrong with me when I went to Uncle's farm. Eventually I was diagnosed with hay fever. It was so bad that I went there less, spending more time at home, sneezing with sore eyes and running nose. I had got into the habit of buying a packet of sherbet with my sweet ration money to eat on a Saturday afternoon while watching the village cricket team but that came to an end due to the long grass. To top it all, I unfortunately missed the departure of Sally the calf.

Sally had grown rapidly in her new outdoor environment though she seemed to get bit over- excited when I went to visit her and I decided that, for her safety, I should keep away. She would not only run around at high speed before rushing up to me but would look for ways of escape for a while afterwards. I was never in danger, she just wanted to be loved but her long field had a public footpath running through it and for the villagers who used it, it was a different matter. As soon as Sally espied someone in her field, her natural instinct, due to the influence of Gerald and I, was to run at speed toward the newcomer. She was now getting quite big and heavy with the result that a member of the public would sometimes get knocked over. This did not go down very well with the people who needed to use the path and Uncle received many complaints. He explained the reason for her actions but the majority were still frightened by her. Eventually she was ready to be sold at market, so off she went. Uncle had previously said she was so big that she would finish up as beef but, to his delight and especially mine, she sold as a milker.

Amongst all the comings and goings of normal village life, a visit by an Ealing Studios film crew might provide a short term lift but our family experienced its own celebrations. The first family wedding in my memory was that of Uncle Bob and Aunt Muriel. I was much too young to join in with the adults but I can well remember the many smiling faces and happy chatter. I believe it was the day that Aunt May met Uncle Alf, my Aunt Muriel's brother. They got on so well together that their friendship turned into courtship which I am happy to say turned into marriage. During this happy relationship they both worked to get Auntie more mobile. To start with, Auntie would walk a short distance to Uncle's house in the village. As she got stronger they increased the distance until the happy day came when she was fit enough to walk the whole way. When they first met, my brother and I were staying at Mill Cottage. We would lie in bed listening to them making loud noises by blowing blades of grass fixed between their fingers and then laughing about it. Gran told us to stay in bed and not look out of the window, maybe they were having a kiss and a cuddle as well. Uncle Alf was a very keen cyclist so it was no surprise to me when they acquired a tandem. Many times I witnessed them setting off from Mill Cottage. They did short journeys to start with and, as their expertise, stamina and confidence grew, they embarked on longer trips. On at least one of our trips to the seaside, going with Gran in Uncle Fred's car, they set off before us. We passed them about half way and waited for their arrival. The speed at which they did that trip greatly impressed me at the time and still does.

Nobody in the world deserved the happiness of her wedding day more than Aunt May. She had been Mum and Dad's bridesmaid and stayed with Mum and me at weekends when Dad was away during the war because Mum became depressed. Mum and I would wait in Trowbridge park for her to emerge from the nursery where she worked and join us during her midday break. Sitting on that park bench, waiting for my favourite aunt to appear, was always the best part of going to town. It gave everyone great joy to celebrate her very happy day. Someone in the family hung a banner on the front of the house with the words 'Just Married' to greet them when they came back off their honeymoon. They were a kindly and generous couple. My brother and I, along with a cousin David, were invited into their house on a Friday to watch cowboy programmes on their television. Being that nobody else in the family had a television this new feature in our lives was looked forward to with great relish. In later years I was given the honour of being godfather to their second son, Vivian. Their marriage, shared with their sons, Terence and Vivian, always seemed to me like a fairy tale come true. Life can be good at times.

Another momentous step in our family's history was Uncle David's long awaited entry into the Royal Air Force. He was the youngest of Dad's family, too young to have previously gone to war. For some time he had been fascinated by aircraft, civil and military. In fact for a long time he had purchased a regular magazine on the subject, accumulating quite a pile of them. Gran told me about his first flight in an aircraft, a very exciting day for him. The plane was going along quite fast, it then banked and turned. Uncle naturally leant away from that turn to feel balanced. He looked out of the window as he did so and to his horror the wing of the plane disappeared. As the plane straightened out so did Uncle and to his huge relief the wing came back into view. Life is full of surprises.

At the age of thirteen, when my hay fever first appeared, I became very unhappy about the effect it was having on me. I found that Uncle's farm was not a good place to be in summer time. Uncle Harold could see my problem and the fact that I was losing my enthusiasm for helping out. We both agreed I should stay away from all that grass and pollen until a cure was found but there never has been one. It was not only Uncle's farm, Mill Cottage and the surrounding countryside that I now had to avoid during the nicest time of the year; it also meant missing the people. I also felt a bit lost without the old regular routine though I knew it would not be permanent.

Uncle can only be described as a proper godfather. He not only made my time on the farm very worthwhile and interesting, he also kept a fatherly eye on my brother and me to make sure we actually survived. On top of that, he and Aunt Louise welcomed us to their home at the nearby hamlet of Friary. In the early years they lived in a wooden bungalow which I remember was quite warm when I slept there on summer nights. They later moved into a more comfortable stone cottage down by the river. Their son David, a few years younger than us, was a great playmate for Gerald and I. Ann, his younger sister, was also welcome company along with the other young children from the hamlet - Brian, Leslie, Janet and last but by no means least, little Enid. It was a great place for us youngsters to play; in fact it seemed a unique, special and almost magical place. I always enjoyed my visits. We stayed within the immediate area of the hamlet, not even going near Uncle's farm which was almost a quarter of a mile away. Daytime was good but night time was another world. Friary had no electricity or gas; the house lighting in Friary Cottage was paraffin lamps hung from the ceilings. I found getting to sleep at night difficult at times, there was only one road leading to Friary and from it rough tracks led to the six houses, so there was no through-traffic noises. The quietness at night left room to hear the nocturnal animals going about their business. Hooting owls we recognised but cousin David explained that some of the other noises were foxes and especially badgers who were very busy bees.

Chapter 8

Work, play and education

As well as moving on from Uncle's farm I had moved on in my school life too. Combe Down Secondary Modern shook me to the core. After being one of the oldest boys in junior school I was now one of the youngest at my new place of education. On my first day, looking around me and witnessing the rough toughness of the older established boys, my heart sank. I was not a happy chappy. In fact I had a bad migraine and had to be taken home. Pride made me determined to give as good as I got. My natural stubbornness then kicked in. Discipline was very strict and prefects were appointed to help keep good order. On the whole I grew up very quickly and along the way I made some good friends. I really enjoyed the lessons. The teachers were excellent but Mr Jones the headmaster had an added talent. He was the man one visited when one got the cane for stepping out of line. To me it was always punishment for crime, in other words, justice. It should never have been phased out. I must admit to being caned a few times. I never felt that I had been wronged but still, that cane really stung.

Gardening at school was a new found pleasure. We all had our own plots but mine was full of flowers. The other plots were for vegetables but, as Mum and Dad said, you can't eat flowers. Try as I might I couldn't get my hands on a vegetable plot. The one lesson I really enjoyed was carpentry. We travelled to Peasedown School by coach for this. We thought our school was hard but on arriving at the mid-day play time we would stand outside the woodwork

February 1953

classroom and watch someone knock six bells out of one of their classmates. There always seemed to be a fight going on. We stayed together hoping that the theory of strength in unity would work. It seemed to. The woodwork class with Mr Sparks was an experience I really enjoyed. To start with, we made wooden joints. The test was to get them fitting together well and we were awarded marks out of ten. My marks were always about nine but I actually achieved the magic mark of ten on one occasion. At the end of the course I was so pleased to make and take home a bedside cabinet and a small oak table which pleased Mum and Dad no end.

Even though ours was a school of hard knocks, there was still a place for honour and respect. To openly fight with one another usually ended up with a teacher's rebuke or, in bad cases, the cane. A tradition that had been passed down through the years resolved a certain problem. If two boys had a real grievance, and wished to come to grips with one another, a special fight would take place at the midday play time. It was a proper boxing match. The playground was out of sight of the school building and it was a boys only playground. A ring was formed by the pupils who also acted as the fair play referee. The two protagonists fought until one was unable to carry on or said that enough was enough. Whatever happened they both had to shake hands at the finish. Those fights were few and I never needed to take part in one but sometimes the sheer ferocity was frightening.

We never had a sports field. Our football was played in the local park, the Firs. For my last couple of years our school was allowed to use another school's ground. We travelled to Timsbury by coach and the trip was really worth it. Football, cricket and athletics were so much easier to play on a nice flat surface. We were able to let ourselves go and sometimes surprised ourselves. We had some brilliant footballers in our school though unfortunately I was not one of them. But, as the saying goes, it's taking part that counts and I certainly enjoyed taking part. In my last year I was appointed as a prefect for the St George team. Every pupil at the school was a member of one of the four teams. George of England, Andrew of Scotland, Patrick of Ireland and David of Wales were the names of the house that competed with each other during the week. On doing well in class, pupils could amass points which were then allotted to their. At the end of the week the house with the most points had a special honour. On the following Monday morning the head of the winning team got to turn the torch that was erected in the main hall so that their saint's name faced all and sundry for the next week. When I eventually became head of St George's house, I was so proud when I was able to place the torch in my team's favour. The whole procedure instilled the value of team effort into pupils, that no matter how good one is personally, more can often be achieved working together.

My last day at the school was also the last day of the school in that building as a new school had been built on the outskirts of Combe Down. I must have done well as a prefect for, to my surprise, I was made Head Boy. With this position went the task of reading to the whole school at the service held at the end of that last day was, I found, quite daunting. To be honest, I was almost lost for words. About a year earlier I was still struggling with my summer course of hay fever especially as there was no medication around to help alleviate my suffering. I still visited Mill Cottage and my favourite country haunts but after a long school day I found myself a bit shattered and my visits were confined to Saturdays only. By now Mum and Dad had bought a television. Evening time found us all riveted to this new entertainment. We were all growing up fast, eating more and growing out of our clothes. We never saw much of

Dad because he was always working and Mum had a very busy day as well. Although they never grumbled, I knew being the eldest I should try to find a way to help, no matter how small.

The answer came one day when I was arriving home on the school coach. A couple of a hundred yards back from the drop off point, on the other side of the main road was a very large chicken farm. It was the start of the school summer holiday. Hay fever or not, I decided to try my luck. Instead of going home, I walked up the driveway to the farm and was lucky enough to find the owner in his office. Maurice Millard seemed quite amused when I came straight out and asked him for a job. Although he must have been caught off his guard he was good enough to say yes; 'Come up next Saturday morning and we will see what can be done for you'. I was to work four hours on a Saturday morning and as many as I could safely manage in the school holidays. I was just a few weeks from being fourteen but I felt much older as I turned up for my first day. Unfortunately that first day was spent in the shed that housed chicken incubators, alongside regular worker Janet, a young lady who lived opposite me and knew me well. It might have been a harmonious start except for one snag. Maurice Millard's Peipards Farm was best known for the sale of day old chicks which had to be transported in small cardboard boxes. My role that day was to empty the returned boxes of the old hay bedding and dust and put in the new hay bedding. My hay fever was the last thing I needed, I sneezed almost continuously, my nose ran a lot and my eyes became so itchy that I couldn't stop rubbing them. Even though my eyes puffed up and I felt completely miserable, I still struggled on until the end of my four hours. The next Saturday was the same. At the end of my shift I had the sympathy of Janet and Maurice. It was painfully obvious that the job was not for me.

Thankfully Maurice was good enough to find me other work. It could also have been my accident with the fire extinguisher that helped to swing it. At one stage during the second morning, when Janet had left me to it, I ran out of boxes. Instead of sitting still and waiting for Janet's return I noticed the fire extinguisher hanging on the wall. Curiosity got the better of me and I took it down. As I did so the metal guard on the bottom, protecting the knob that had to be struck to start it, came off. As I bent quickly down to retrieve it, the knob struck the ground and off it went. There was no way I could stop it. I tried but my luck was out. All I could do was stand there and watch the room fill up with foam. When Janet came back, I was still trying to figure out what I could do with it all. I panicked and told Maurice that it had started on its own. Even though I am sure he didn't believe me, he was good enough to give me another chance. The only thing I missed about that job was being able to watch the chicks hatch and take their first steps. Janet also kindly let me handle them, though I had to try hard not to sneeze on them.

The work on a farm could be very hard in those days. Mechanisation was a boon but it couldn't be used for every job. There was always a lot to do from dawn to dusk. Peipard farm's staff all worked with a will and took their work seriously. The thing that took me a bit by surprise was the jokes and good natured pranks that went on to make that hard work more bearable. Edgar, for instance, would splash cold water on our backs when we were least expecting it. The fact that we had been out in the fields with our shirts off, in the hot sun getting a tan or burning, greatly increased the shock and his amusement. The mess room was a revelation during tea breaks. There, world affairs, village gossip and each other's problems were all discussed at length along with friendly banter. The pin-up pictures on the walls were a real eye opener as well. Some of the jokes were very rude and I didn't fully understand them at first but my education soon improved in that respect.

One of the Saturday morning jobs involved the cleaning of small portable chicken houses called hay boxes. These served as nurseries for the young chicken to grow up in. We used stiff bristled hand brushes and hosepipes. It was a hard, boring and wet job that narrowly beat creosoting as a chore. Everything wooden that housed livestock had to be creosoted at some time or another. The strong smell of creosote would follow me everywhere and getting it on one's clothes was not a clever thing to do. Not all of it was put on with brushes; there was also a dipping and spraying machine, driven by a petrol engine which built up pressure in a combustion chamber. It had two front wheels and handles that enabled it to be pushed like a wheel barrow. It was a very fast and efficient way of creosoting but I soon learned that spraying into the wind could have dire consequences. One of the regular workers, Sid, had a nasty accident and I was the cause. On helping him to dip some large heavy sections of chicken houses into the dipping tank, I stupidly let my end drop too soon and splashed Sid in the face. Creosote burns and two eyes-full put Sid in a great deal of pain. We were both panicking a lot but I helped guide him down to Maurice. Thankfully he was there and managed to get Sid to open his eyes enough to pour liquid paraffin in. Fortunately the treatment worked and Sid had no need to go to hospital. All the same, he was lucky not to get seriously damaged that day. All I could do was apologise which I kept doing, much to Sid's annoyance. Another lesson hard learned. It was one of the most terrifying moments of my life.

Shortly after this, I was given the task of creosoting the exterior of the barn doors. Just as I had erected a ladder and proceeded with the brushwork, it decided to snow. The snow came down thick and fast and by the time I was a quarter of the way down the doors, the yard was covered. On turning around to admire it, I must have moved the base of the ladder a little because it sped backwards across the yard like a sledge. The top of the ladder slid down the door with me balanced on it. By the time I hit the ground I was in a kneeling position. The pain was indescribable and the bruising was so bad that it was many days before I could walk properly again. Fortunately nothing was broken. At that time my mind was split between my pain and the picture I had painted. On hitting the ground, the almost full can of creosote had distributed its contents everywhere. The contrast of the black creosote on the white looked like a crazy Picasso painting. I managed to freewheel home on my bicycle, luckily downhill all the way, and I was required to finish the job on the next Saturday. I was grateful it didn't snow that day.

Egg collecting was done in bulk as a lot of the hen houses were in large fields some way from the farm and needed a tractor and trailer to fetch them. As I couldn't drive, I seldom helped with this task, just being called upon at busy times. Stanley, a self-employed plumber who was a regular egg collector, helped out a lot when his other customers could spare him and also kept the plumbing shipshape on the farm. He was an easy going, pleasant man, always ready with a smile and upbeat praise, the sort of man that one couldn't help liking. He took great pride in his work but was restricted with an arthritic hip which needed surgery later on in his life. One afternoon during his collection he parked the tractor and trailer laden with buckets of eggs at the top of a field. For some reason, while he was in a hen house the tractor and trailer started to move on its own. Stanley was quite startled when it passed the open doorway. By this time it had gathered a great deal of speed. Poor Stan never stood a chance of catching it. The field was steep and at the bottom was a dry stone wall bordered by trees and bushes. Beyond that was a wide track with a wooded area beyond it. The tractor went faster and faster, scattering unsuspecting chickens on the way and missing all the houses. The stone wall didn't stop the runaway, just slowed it down a little. The loaded trailer followed the tractor through the hole in the wall and came to a sudden stop as the tractor shot across the track and embedded itself in the bank on the other side. The buckets of eggs did not stop. The eggs decorated the trees and tractor, the yolk really was on Stanley that day. He had his leg pulled for a while afterwards but not within earshot of the boss. Because of the age and condition of the tractor, Stan was found to be not fully at fault. The wildlife didn't care. It was amazing how quickly they cleared those eggs away.

The problem of fowl pest meant that testing took place every year and needless to say, I was roped in to help. By this time I had been joined on the labour force by Robert, my friend and next door neighbour. He was a breath of fresh air, always cheerful and not afraid of hard work. The saying that a problem shared is a problem halved was certainly true in our case. Because every chicken had to be tested, it took some of the staff away from their everyday duties so speed and efficiency were important. Robert and I were put into each chicken house to catch the inhabitants who hadn't been let out that morning and were probably getting a bit anxious. We took it in turns to catch the chickens while other members of the team stood just inside the door waiting for someone to open it and take those chickens, two at a time, for testing. Catching them was easy enough. We used a long piece of stiff wire with a hook on the end, which when hooked around the chicken's legs and feet made it easy to pull them out from under the dropping board where they chose to hide from us. Holding onto a pair of legs of an upside down chicken in each hand took its toll on our arms and shoulders. The really hard part of that job was the effect of a chicken flapping its wings, very powerful things those wings. The dust would rise from the floor in clouds, making us cough and sneeze, in addition to which it tended to stick to the substantial amount of sweat on our foreheads. There were always a lot of flies on the ceilings in the summer which took to flying around when those wildly flapping wings frightened them. We kept our mouths shut as much as possible and were hugely relieved to step out into the fresh air.

On the last day of testing, in the second year, some joker told Robert and me that we would have to be tested too. Knowing it was highly unlikely, us not being chickens susceptible to fowl pest, we in the end relented. Hoping this would be another leg pull, the serious faces of the testers did make us think, in the back of our minds, 'what if? What then?' as we bared our arms. Robert went first while I looked away. After taking a sample of his blood and placing it on the slide, I became startled by a cry of 'Oh no!' They told me later that my face was a picture and to top it all they never let on that Robert was okay. They went ahead with my test, trying hard not to burst out laughing. Apparently it was not the first time they had done it to some poor unsuspecting young farm worker. It was a great pity I never had the chance to get my revenge the following year. Another prank was pulled when I had to help remove heavy sacks of corn from one of the sheds. Under the neck of one of them we found a family of small mice. The other men told me that normally they were required to kill them. Instead, one of the men put them into the empty lunchbox of one of his colleagues. Nobody found out who opened the box when he got home or what happened to the mice; the subject was never mentioned.

One of the jobs I enjoyed was de-stoning a very large field ready for crops to be sown. Several men followed a slow moving tractor and trailer, backward and forward, throwing all the loose stones in to the trailer. Even the driver was able to take part but accuracy was highly important. Nobody wanted to be hit by another man's stone. Teamwork was the key, nobody hurried and at the end of the allotted time it was amazing how many trailers we had filled. Working together like that gave me a feel good factor on the day. It also gave me a huge backache the next day. An outbreak of foot and mouth broke out in various parts of the country while I was at Peipards Farm. Mr Millard had cattle so special precautions had to be taken and large containers of disinfectant were placed at each entrance to the farm. Everybody entering or leaving had to dip in their wellington-booted feet. Fortunately foot and mouth never came to the farm.

I was very happy to re-acquaint myself with Maurice's Yellow Labrador dog. Four years earlier it had entered the village school playground at dinner break time. The dog had seemingly wandered from the farm about half a mile away and must have been attracted by the crowd of friendly young children. After a time, the dog must have had enough and decided to leave but found itself surrounded with no way out. The only way was to make a break for it but, unfortunately, I was in the way. I was well and truly knocked over and sustained some cuts and grazes from the impact when I landed. By this time the teachers had realised what was going on. They caught the dog and found Mr Millard's name and address on its collar. On arriving at the school, Maurice and the teachers questioned me about my injuries. My answer let the dog off the hook. If it had bitten me it would have been more serious but Maurice and his dog were able to go home with a clear conscience. Now, after all that time, Maurice had remembered the incident and arranged a special meeting for both of us. He took us both down to his car garage and asked me to clean and tidy while keeping Mr Labrador with me for the afternoon, as he and his wife were going out. The afternoon went well. The dog had a really good nature. It was friendly but not over the top. He didn't even get bored and try to wander off. From then until I left the farm we were good friends, although he remained steadfastly the boss's dog and seldom left his side. In fact if you saw the Labrador you could be sure that Maurice was not far behind.

Near the end of my time there I realised that farming was not for me. Hay fever was one reason; the other was that a farm was not an animal sanctuary but a business. A hard fact of life is that some of those animals provide food for us. I saw how humanely the workers looked after the animals in their care. It must have been a bit of a wrench if one of those workers became attached to an animal that had to be sold, for whatever purpose. I had asked the staff a few times about this scenario but always got the same answer: 'You don't let that happen'. Personally, I have always been a big softie and got into the habit of trying to make friends with many of the animals that I have met. Despite being extremely hard work cleaning out the one battery hen house gave us all a great deal of pleasure because it meant the occupants got a holiday. While we scrubbed the place down with stiff bristled brushes and hosepiped it as we went, the hens were taken to another part of the farm and stayed there until the place had dried out. Unfortunately for them they had to return. That was another thing I was not at all happy about. I did however witness a story with a happy ending.

My only period of time working Peipards Farm around Christmas saw me working in the plucking shed. It was a hard job for young fingers and overall I didn't enjoy it. On the last day someone brought in a duck, saying it had been ordered and could we see to it. The duck stood in the middle of the room looking around. It obviously didn't like what it saw because it shot off at great sped to the corner of the room where the plucking machine was situated. The heavy metal machine was bolted to the floor and wall and wasn't used much. The duck dived around the back of it and remained there for the rest of the day. Everybody except me tried to get it out, without success. It would have taken up too much valuable working time to remove the machine so, at the end of the day, we left food and water for Mrs Duck, locked the door to keep out predators, and went home for Christmas. On the first day back, during dinner break time, we were having a great time relating our holiday experiences when during a lull in the chatter we heard a quite different noise. We looked at each other thinking that someone had suddenly decided to make animal noises. One of the brighter ones in the room came up with the answer, 'It's that duck!' We had all been guilty of forgetting the duck on that first morning back but would it run away again? One didn't have to be clever to realise that it might be hungry so a broken-up sandwich was thrown in first. It was too busy eating it to notice the man who picked it up. The mess room was in the same building as the plucking shed, divided by a thin wooden partition. That fact enabled us to hear the quacking which was lucky for the duck. It proved doubly lucky as Bert the foreman and Maurice Millard kindly decided that it had won its freedom. It was put in with the chickens and continued laying eggs after it had put back on the weight it had lost over Christmas.

During the last summer I was there, to save me from the worst ravages of hay fever, I was asked to help out in the Millard's garden. Mrs Millard was very easy to get on with and a great pleasure to work for but gardening was not going to be my chosen profession. One of the lighter moments at the house was the day I was asked to clean out the cellar with Harold, an older man and part-timer. After removing all the bottles and bits of furniture it was just a matter of removing the cobwebs and scrubbing down the walls and floor with stiff bristled brushes and a hosepipe. It was a hard and tiring job but when we finished Mr and Mrs Millard were very pleased with our efforts. There was a very large cask of cider in the middle of the room, impossible to move, so we worked around it. As we sat getting our breath back after we had finished, they told us that the cider in that barrel was quite old and strong, in fact a very good vintage, and we could help ourselves. I was not a drinker but would definitely try some while cider was Harold's favourite drink. We started on our reward. I was teetotal but he was good company and the exquisite taste of the cider ensured that I had a good amount. Feeling the full effects, I said goodnight and thank you and made my wobbly way home on my bike, glad again that it was all downhill. Harold stayed on, enjoying his favourite brew but had to be taken home by car. I wonder if he slept as soundly as I did that night.

I never, ever found out who gave Robert and me a shock with the electric fence that was used to keep the cattle in place in the fields. When it was turned down to its lowest setting, it only gave a small shock and Robert and I would show off by holding it as long as we could. The medium setting commanded and got respect while the highest setting was something to be avoided. This was not normally used, only for the odd member of the cattle community who thought escaping was a good idea. My first experience of that high setting was a real shocker. I believe it was meant to be. After moving some of the fence posts without turning off the power - a move made possible by the insulators on them - I touched the wire just to make sure all was well. The shock of that high setting sent my hand up under my chin. I hit myself so hard that I bit into my tongue which at that moment was hanging out. I was sore in more ways than one for quite a few days. Robert was also a victim but we never caught the joker. It gave me a huge respect for electricity and probably saved me from harm in my later career in the building trade.

Eventually my time at the farm came to an end. I was a bit loath to say goodbye to the Millards and a great bunch of workmates but most of them lived in the village so it was not goodbye forever. I left there, as I left school, knowing that I had learned a lot, not only education-wise but in terms of human nature too. I was also a bit relieved to have survived the course. My Dad found me a job with one of the two building firms in the village. Jim and Buster Male ran the firm of Male and Marchant. They were giving me a chance as my Grandad Lintern had worked there in their younger days. One of his skills was as a blacksmith. They said that if I was half as good as he was I would be okay. Mum and Dad had arranged a week's family holiday but first of all I was to work a week's trial.

My first day should go down in history. It was certainly a day I have never forgotten. The firm was well into building a small house attached to the house next door. My first task was to assist Chris Pearce who was building the block walls. Using his tools, I cut the big blocks down to smaller sizes as needed, trying hard not to get things wrong. Unfortunately I dropped his wooden rule down between the house wall and the cut down edge of the lawn. Silly me. On dropping down to retrieve it, one foot landed on top of it and broke it. Chris was not amused and informed me that I would have to buy one of my own, as well as replacing his. All I could promise was that I would when I got paid. Fortunately he kept me on as his mate but more was to follow. Later on in the morning I happened to glance at the road on the other side of the wall as a rather fast car went up the hill. To my horror, as it did so, a black cat on the other side of the road made a dash to beat the car. The car ran over the cat which to my surprise immediately got up and ran down the path of the house behind us. On hearing this, the other workers told me that the man who owned that house also owned the land and the house we were working on. Being that I was the only witness I should go and tell what I knew. On arriving at the house I found the cat in a very bad way. The owner, on seeing the poor animal, decided there and then to put it out of its misery. After etching his shotgun he suggested that I should go back and prepare my colleagues for the inevitable. We heard the gun go off and kept as quiet as we could for the rest of the day. Just to complete my day, I stepped on the end of a board that served as a makeshift floor in the upper part of the house. It should have been resting on a floor joist but my luck wasn't in that day. The end of the board went down and so did I. Luckily I was facing the right and my hips got wedged between the joists instead of me going down to the ground floor. My workmates said I was lucky but the grazing of my hips put me in two minds. They apologised for the error and I promised not to tell the boss. I went home that night slightly traumatised. My parents consoled me by promising that not every day would be so bad. The rest of the week went well although mastering the art of mixing every bucket of plaster to the same consistency for Ken the plasterer was not as easy as it looked. At the end of the week off went our family for our holiday to a camping site near Bournemouth.

Mum, Dad and six children in tents seemed a bit ambitious especially as we hadn't attempted anything like it before. It was probably all we could afford in those days. My parents must have prayed for fine weather. Their prayers were answered for most of the week except for one night when the girls' tent blew down and it was raining hard. After vainly trying to put the tent back up, readjustments were made and some of us spent the rest of the night in the car. Miraculously we came through the week in one piece and with a much better understanding of each other. Needless to say tempers did fray at times but overall I think we enjoyed that last big holiday together. The final day at the beach was my fifteenth birthday. We were all sat quietly in the large car when a wheel appeared in front of us and carried on down the road. Dad's voice broke the silence when he said 'I think that's ours'. Nobody disagreed as we came slowly to a stop. We were all seated in such an orderly way that the car was evenly balanced and didn't seem to miss the runaway wheel. We had been going downhill in a quiet road so no other traffic was involved. Dad gingerly got out without mishap, told us all to sit still and went to get help. We got back to camp late and tired and slept like logs. The car was towed back and replaced for another the next day which served as our transport home. Over that following weekend Dad found out for me that I was to be an employee of Male and Marchant. The next sixteen and a half years were to become the most informative and happy days of my working life. It helped to have good bosses, customers who appreciated me and brilliant workmates. Money is okay, it's essential to live on, but the greatest, richest thing one can have it a loving, caring family and all of my life up to now I have been so lucky to have an abundance of that. That's what I call a privilege in life.

Acknowledgements

My heartfelt thanks to Pam and Ivor Slocombe for their enthusiastic vote of confidence and all their hard work, together with their daughter-in-law Dr Kate Ferry, in the preparation of this book.

I also owe thanks to the late Alan Dodge and his wife Margaret for their initial encouragement, and to Roger Jones who read my first efforts and has now published my latest, and to the Freshford and District Local History Society for their generous sponsorship of this publication.

Also available from Ex Libris Press ~

FRESHFORD: *The History of a Somerset Village*
by Alan Dodge
Perhaps one of the most comprehensive, well written and clearly presented village histories ever to have appeared in print. The fruit of many years research and fascination with his home village.
A newly revised edition, published in 2014
285 pages; illustrated throughout, Indexed; Price £12.00

Also by Alan Dodge:
FROM TURNPIKE GATES TO CHRISTMAS WAITS
Historical Notes from Village Life
In no planned sequence, for seven years Alan Dodge wrote a brief historical note for the parish magazine which generally arose out of some observation or seasonal change. Delightful and enlightening reading.
96 pages; Illustrated; Price £5.95

Two books of local walks which both feature Freshford and its environs:

WHERE WILTSHIRE MEETS SOMERSET
20 best walks around Bath, Bradford on Avon, Trowbridge, Westbury, Warminster and Frome
by Roger Jones
Latest edition of a book which has been continually in print and updated since 1982.
128 pages; sketch maps and illustrations; Price £7.95

BEYOND WHERE WILTSHIRE MEETS SOMERSET
20 more best walks [as above] plus Box and Corsham
by Roger Jones
A second collection of local walks first published in 2015
128 pages; sketch maps and illustrations; Price £7.95

Books available via your local bookshop, from The Galleries in Freshford or via our website, post-free.
To view our full list of books on Wiltshire and Somerset please visit www.ex-librisbooks.co.uk